Leonidas Papadakis

Training Periodization
for maximizing soccer performance

An effective practical
training model

© 2019 Sportbook Publications
ISBN 978-618-5316-48-8

Photos by Shutterstock.com, Christian Bertrand / Shutterstock.com,
Mitch Gunn / Shutterstock.com, Ververidis Vasilis / Shutterstock.com, cristiano barni / Shutterstock.com
Paolo Bona / Shutterstock.com, A.RICARDO / Shutterstock.com

SPORTBOOK Publications
Thessaloniki, Andrea Papandreou 172, 56626, Greece
Tel: (+30) 2310.629319
http://www.sportbook.gr
e-mail: info@sportbook.gr

All rights reserved. No part of this publication may be reproduced, stored in a retrieval system, or transmitted in any form or by any means, electronic, mechanical, photocopy, recording or otherwise, without prior written permission of the copyright owner. Nor can it be circulated in any form of binding or cover other than that in which it is published and without similar condition including this condition being imposed on a subsequent purchaser.

*To the coaches who teach me, the players who tolerate me,
my family that supports me and to Dimitra who inspires me every day.*

CONTENTS

PROLOGUE 7

PART A: PERFORMANCE 8
Physical abilities 11
Technical abilities 21
Tactical abilities 31
Cognitive and psychological abilities 33
Synopsis 34

PART B: SEASON 36
Transition Period 39
Preparation Period 42
Competitive Period 43
"Breaking down" the system 48
Wave-like mathematical sequence 56

PART C: PHYSICAL ABILITIES 58
Endurance 60
"Wave-like" sequence of endurance training stimuli 69
Strength 71
Speed 81
Synopsis 86

PART D: PLANNING **90**
Example of a complete weekly micro cycle for the Endurance Block........... 97
Example of a complete weekly micro cycle for the Strength Block............ 109
Example of a complete weekly micro cycle for the Speed Block.............. 121
Example of a complete weekly micro cycle training for the Maintenance Block . 133
Example of a complete weekly micro cycle for the Recovery Block 145

BIBLIOGRAPHY 156

PROLOGUE

I often find myself having conversations with friends and colleagues, searching for the reasons why soccer is so unique and stands apart from all the other sports. I sincerely apologize to all my colleagues in the world of sports, but soccer simply cannot be compared to any other. To the entire world soccer is considered the king of sports, but for some it is much more than that. Anyone can play it, regardless of their social status, anyone can voice their opinion regardless of their background in training, anyone can relate to their idol regardless of their age and it can even form political identities and in extreme cases, fanaticism. Soccer awakes emotions, alters moods and gives meaning to the next day. All this is born from the unpredictable nature of the sport at every moment of the game as well as the final outcome that it will bring. For those who are weak, the right to dream of victory is a right that they might only have in the sport of soccer.

This unpredictability of variable circumstances that can not be repeated during the game, as well as the final score, is a result of the player's actions, whether they are following directives or acting independently, in order to succeed in specific to bring specific objectives.

The sum of these separate actions represents the overall performance of each of the players that form the team, and therefore the overall performance of the team itself. Therefore the need to improve and stabilize the performance of each player during the annual season is what urged me to search for, apply and write about the Periodic Training Model, which I will analyze and present as simply and well documented as I possibly can.

Leonidas Papadakis

Performance

When carefully analyzing a game or a player individually, we observe patterns of consecutive decisions and actions that create diverse situations both in terms of their approach and their appropriateness. In this way, contacting the ball, being able to predict a situation, the ability for quick decision-making, speed, endurance, player positioning etc. compose a puzzle. A puzzle that progressively, and while constantly altering the possible outcome, will reveal the picture of the overall performance.

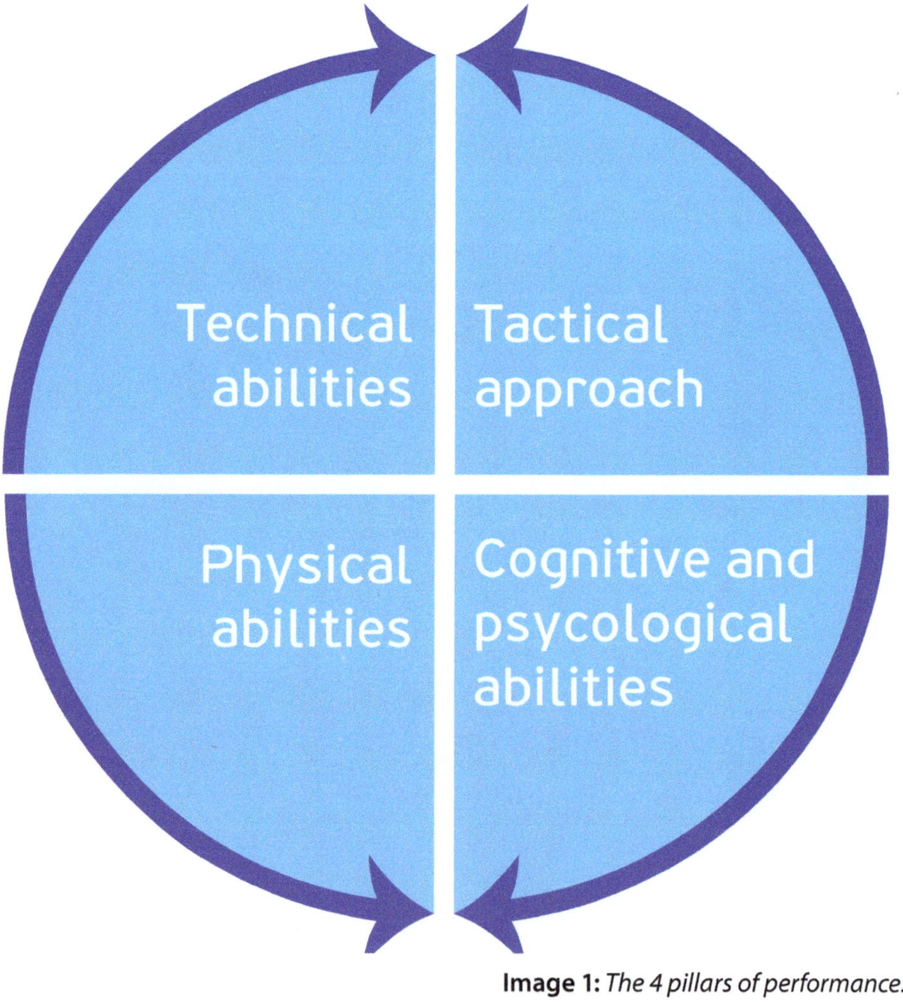

Technical abilities	Tactical approach
Physical abilities	Cognitive and psycological abilities

Image 1: *The 4 pillars of performance.*

These 4 pillars determine the performance of each player (image 1):
- Technical abilities
- Physical abilities
- Tactical abilities
- Cognitive and psycological abilities

Further analyzing these four pillars, we can create a diagram (image 2) containing the main sub-categories. Such a diagram can help us identify potential weaknesses, as well as determine the performance level of each player during training and official games.

Even though the strengths and weaknesses of each player according to the 4 pillars are subjective, it is necessary to create a plan for determining and monitoring these specific skills and abilities. One look at such a plan makes us realize how complicated it is to determine if "it was a good game" for a player and that many factors affect his performance.

Imagine if during a game you could press pause at any moment and at each one of those moments the player must be able to respond to the various challenges of the subcategories of these four pillars of performance.

Physical abilities

The physical abilities and needs of a player are easy to determine through various monitoring systems available in the market (GPS, heart rate telemetric systems, video analysis). Many teams use technology during training and matches in order to collect data that will help them to determine the current as well as the desired performance level of their players.

In this way, sports scientists around the world have been trying to answer the question "how much and at what level of intensity?" which is one of the daily concerns the coaching team needs to address in order to design the right schedules for each training cycle as well as for the entire competitive season.

One of the most commonly methods used is through heart rate recording during training. Many studies have to record and analyze the internal training load the athletes are experiencing during training (Djaoui et al., 2017; Dellal et

Performance

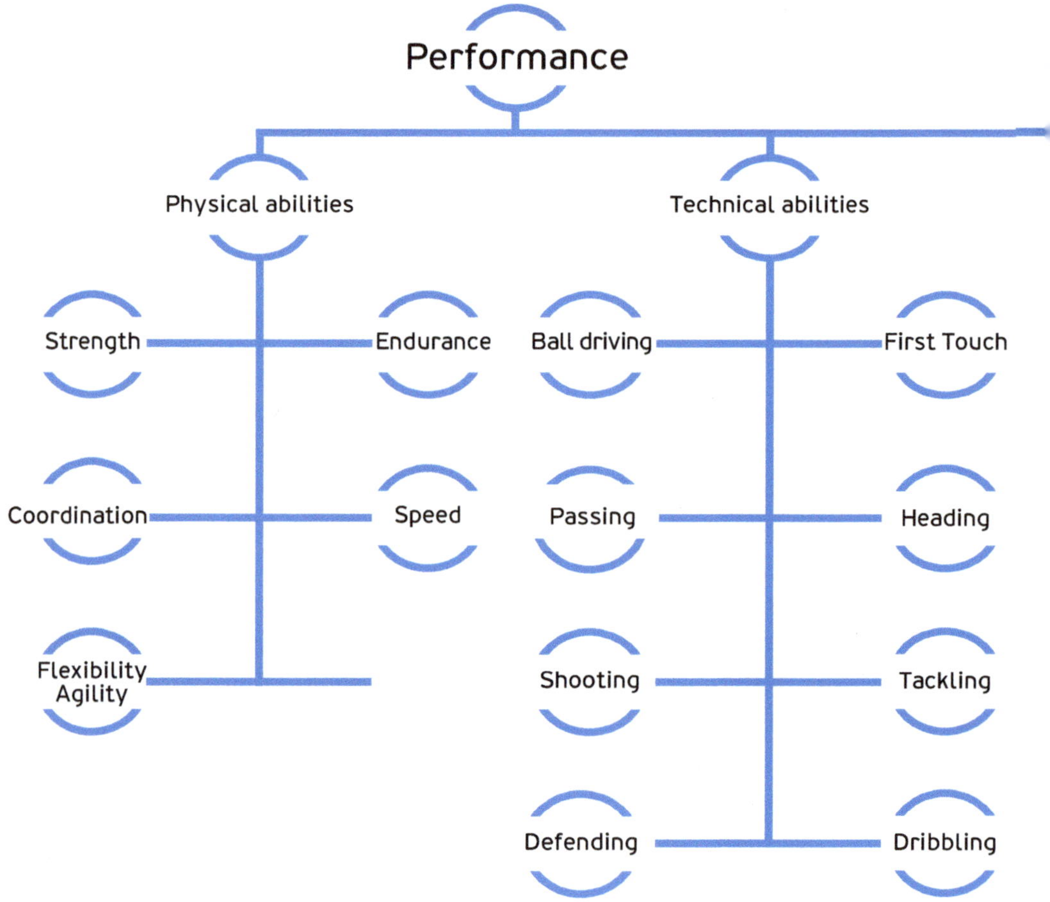

```
                    Performance
                   /           \
         Physical abilities   Technical abilities
          /         \           /         \
      Strength   Endurance   Ball driving  First Touch
      Coordination  Speed    Passing       Heading
      Flexibility           Shooting       Tackling
      Agility
                            Defending      Dribbling
```

Periodization Training Method - Maximizing Performance in Soccer

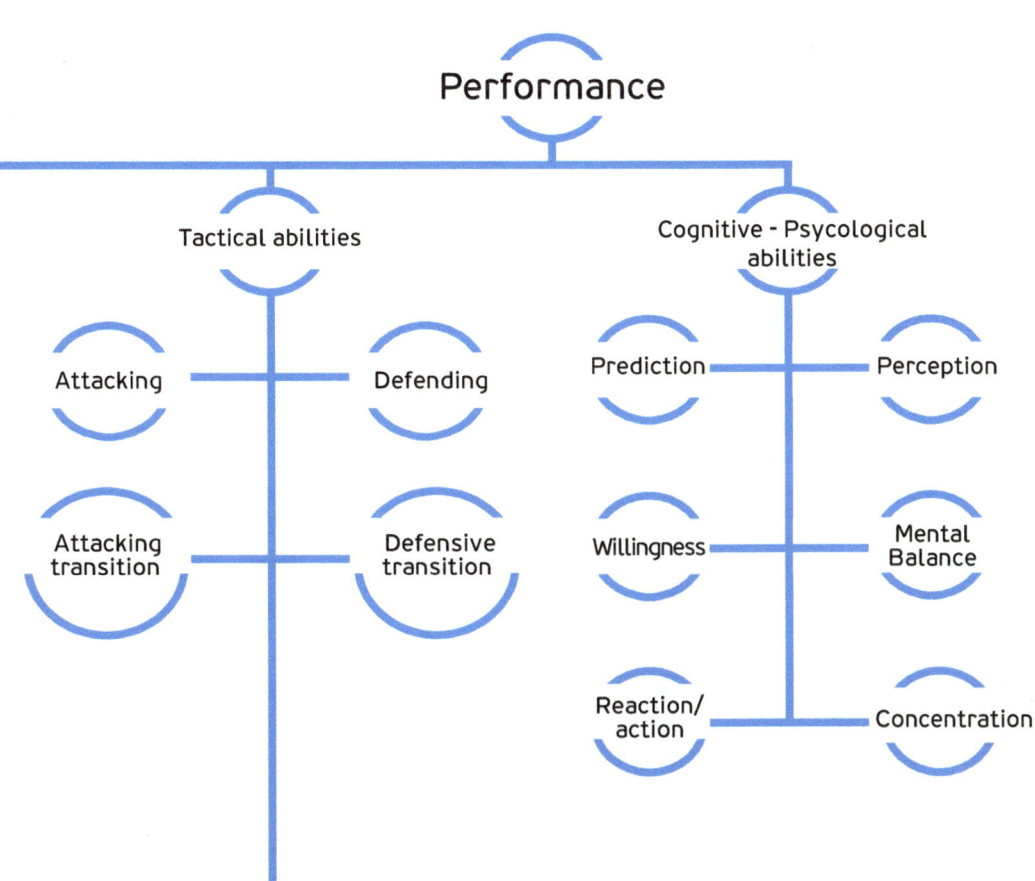

Image 2: *The Four Pillars of Performance.*

A PERFORMANCE

Performance

al., 2012). The last few years though, GPS systems have been developed through which the scientific support teams create data files about the external load that the athlete receives as well (Foster et al., 2017; Sands et al., 2017; Cardinale & Varley, 2017; Malone et al., 2017; Dellasera et al., 2014).

Internal load = physiological and psychological stress as a result of training
External load = the sum of actions that the athlete executed

Various methods have been developed to approach and monitor the training process but the objective is the same for all of them. To determine the most appropriate training and rehabilitation plan in order to achieve the most ideal performance within a specific time frame (Halson, 2014; Jones et al., 2017). Sports scientists are now an integral part of soccer clubs and collaborate closely with the coaching staff in order to create and adjust Periodic Training models for each training phase, depending on their objectives.

An overview of the physical abilities and needs of each player can be provided through a "fitness report" which contains the analysis attained from the official games. Each player, depending on his position, will execute specific actions, always in accordance to their personal level as well as the level of the championship he is participating in, which allows us to both understand his individual needs as well as the type of training we need to be providing for him (Rampinini et al., 2017; Di Salvo et.al., 2009; Bradley et al., 2009; Di Salvo et al., 2013; Bradley et al., 2011; Gregson et al., 2010). What is important is not only the total distance covered by the player but also the intensity in which this distance has been covered (Bush et al., 2015; Barnes et al., 2014). The table presents a comparison of the total distance that a player typically covers as well as the distance covered at various speed thresholds during Premier League versus Champions League games.

	CL (mean ± SD) (95% CI)	PL (mean ± SD) (95% CI)	Effect Size (Cohen's) (95% CI)
total distance	11.102 ± 916 (11.086;11.118)	10.746 ± 964 (10.730;10.762)	-0,38 (-0,40;-0,35)
walking	3.709 ± 260 (3.704;3.713)	3.794 ± 267 3.789;3.798)	0,32 (0,30;0,25)
slow running or jogging	4.468 ± 518 (4.459;4.477)	4.255 ± 594 (4.245;4.264)	-0,38 (0,41;0,36)
high intensity running	1.877 ± 413 (1.870;1.884)	1721 ± 412 (1.714;1.728)	-0,38 (-0,40;-0,35)
very high intensity running	750 ± 222 (746;754)	693 ± 214 (689;696)	-0,22 (-0,29;-0,24)
sprinting	273 ± 125 (271;275)	258 ± 122 (256, 260)	-0,12 (-0,15;0,10)

CL = Championship Leaque, PL: Premier Leaque

For example most research shows that central and wide midfielders cover far more total distance than central and wide defenders and forwards (Bradley et al., 2009; Bradley et al., 2010; Di Salvo et al., 2013). As far as distances covered in high speed is concerned, (>14.4 km/h the above chart is considered high intensity, >19.8 km/h is considered very high intensity running, >25.1 km/h is considered sprinting) research shows that central defenders cover the shortest distance in relation to the other positions (Bradley et al., 2010). Wide midfielders cover significantly higher distances in high intensities compared to all other positions (i.e. >19.8km/h) (Bradley et al., 2009; Di Salvo et al., 2009; Di Salvo et al., 2013), where as for sprinting (>25.1 km/h) wide midfielders cover the highest distances (Bradley et al., 2009; Di Salvo et al., 2009; Di Salvo et al., 2013).

Performance

Image 3: *Basic player positions.*

    Each player position has different demands in relation to the needs of the game with players having variable intensity in the total distance covered per game, as analyzed below with comparative data from Premier League games and Championship games (Bradley et al., 2010; Bradley et al., 2013; Rampinini et al., 2007; Di Salvo et al., 2009; Bradley et al., 2009; Di Salvo et al., 2013; Bradley et al., 2011; Gregson et al., 2010). As a result the training process is tailored and adjusted to the personal needs and abilities of each athlete.

		Forwards (mean ± SD) (95% CI)	Central defenders (mean ± SD) (95% CI)	Central midfielders (mean ± SD) (95% CI)	Wide defenders (Fullbacks) (mean ± SD) (95% CI)	Wide midfielders (mean ± SD) (95% CI)
walking	CL	3.856 ± 266	3.838 ± 202	3.566 ± 231	3.681 ± 219	3.612 ± 265
	PL	3.956 ± 282	3.916 ± 202	3.666 ± 245	3.759 ± 211	3.673 ± 280
	ES	0,38 (0,31;0,44)	0,39 (0,34;0,44)	0,42 (0,37;0,47)	0,36 (0,31;0,41)	0,22 (0,16;0,29)
slow running or jogging	CL	4.151 ± 566	4.231 ± 393	4.890 ± 431	4.394 ± 400	4.645 ± 467
	PL	3.890 ± 675	3.958 ± 414	4.736 ± 516	4.166 ± 389	4.519 ± 537
	ES	-0,42 (-0,48;-0,35)	-0,68 (-0,73;-0,63)	-0,32 (-0,37;-0,27)	-0,58 (-0,63;-0,53)	-0,25 (-0,31;-0,19)
high intensity running	CL	1.700 ± 359	1.525 ± 245	2.218 ± 349	1.861 ± 286	2.151 ± 346
	PL	1.574 ± 355	1.348 ± 231	2.057 ± 332	1.689 ± 248	2.030 ± 382
	ES	-0,35 (-0,42;-0,29)	-0,75 (-0,80;-0,70)	-0,47 (-0,52;-0,42)	-0,65 (-0,70;-0,60)	-0,33 (-0,39;-0,27)
very high intensity running	CL	747 ± 186	540 ± 129	829 ± 199	772 ± 169	955 ± 194
	PL	703 ± 168	482 ± 116	765 ± 191	712 ± 156	898 ± 200
	ES	-0,25 (-0,31;-0,19)	-0,47 (-0,52;-0,42)	-0,33 (-0,38;-0,28)	-0,37 (-0,42;-0,32)	-0,29 (-0,35;-0,23)
sprinting	CL	304 ± 120	180 ± 75	259 ± 105	301 ± 112	382 ± 128
	PL	297 ± 115	168 ± 72	241 ± 106	285 ± 113	353 ± 124
	ES	-0,05 (-0,12;-0,01)	-0,16 (-0,21;-0,11)	-0,17 (-0,22;-0,12)	-0,14 (-0,19;-0,09)	-0,23 (-0,29;-0,17)

CL = Championship League, PL: Premier League, ES: effect size

As a matter of fact, recent data shows that the physical demands of the game have risen the last few years, for example the total distance covered per game has risen by 2% during the last 7 annual seasons (Barnes et al., 2014). An even more recent study from the same research team discovered that this rise concerned the central defenders and central midfielders whilst minimal changes were observed in the other positions (wide defenders and wide midfielders, forwards) (Bush et al., 2015). The same research team also observed that all players, regardless of their position, have covered more distances in high or very high intensity, especially in the case of wide defenders (Bush et al., 2015). What is also interesting is that the team formation, may also affect the physical demands on the players. For example, a comparative study regarding three commonly used formations (4-4-2, 4-3-3, and 4-5-1), revealed that although the total distance covered was similar, the defensive players in the 4-4-2 formation covered more total distance compared to their counterparts in the other formations (Bradley et.al., 2011).

Performance

Image 4: *Formation 4-3-3.*

Image 5: *Formation 4-4-2.*

Image 6: *Formation 4-5-1.*

Furthermore, even though the total distance covered with high/very high intensity running was the same between all formations, the forwards in the 4-3-3 formation covered more distance in high/very high intensity running than the forwards of the 4-5-1 and 4-4-2 formations. The same occurred for the defensive players of the 4-4-2 formation, in comparison to the defensive players of the other formations (Bradley et al., 2011). More "flexible" soccer systems have been developed in recent years bringing forward new studies that attempt to quantify the differences between the physical demands of the new and the classical formations. For example, the total distance covered was significantly lower in the 4-2-3-1 formation as opposed to the 3-5-2 formation, but comparable to the distance covered in the 4-4-2 formation (Tierney et al., 2016). Furthermore, distance covered in high/very intensity running was lower in the 4-2-3-1 compared to the 3-5-2 formation but similar to the 4-4-2 and 3-4-3 formations (Tierney et al., 2016).

Differentiations in levels of intensity or duration alter the energy demanded for the specific activities, which could result in the athlete's fatigue (Bradley & Noakes, 2013). The energy the athletes require is supplied by the interaction of the three energy supply systems.

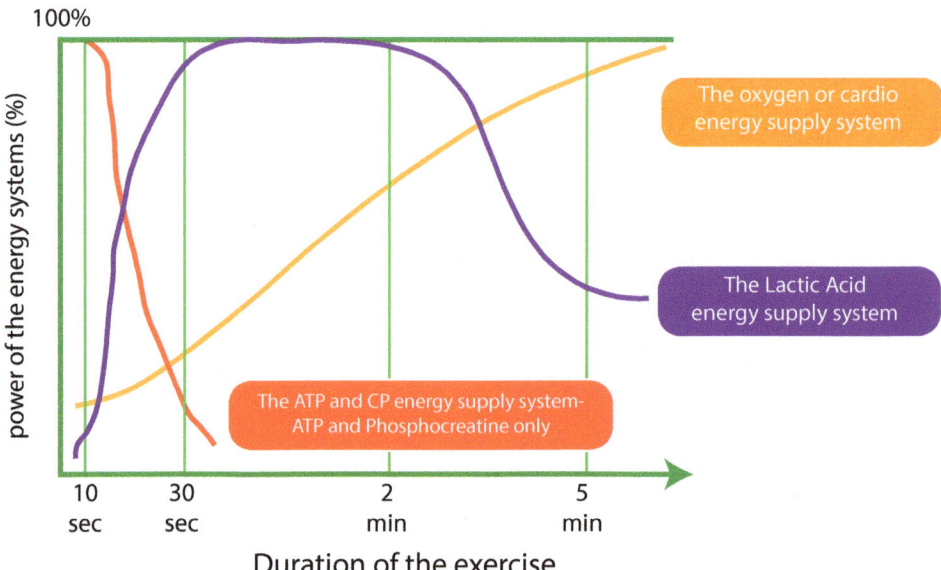

Image 7: *Athlete energy demands and interaction of the 3 energy supply systems.*

1. **The ATP/CP system -** ATP and Phosphocreatine only
   - The total amount of energy supplied through this system is limited but is provided at very high rates.
   - This energy supply system prevails when extreme efforts are made for a period of time of maximum 7 seconds.

2. **The Lactic Acid system -** Carbohydrates only
   - The energy provided through this system is average.
   - This energy supply system prevails when efforts are made for a period of time from 7 seconds until 1 minute.

3. **The aerobic or cardio system -** Carbohydrates, fat, protein
   - The total amount of energy supplied through this system is large but is provided at low rates.
   - This energy supply system prevails when efforts are made for a period of time of 1 minute and onwards, regardless of the level of intensity.

The above differences in regard to the physical demands of the game, could possibly lead to differentiations in the way that each energy system participates in the supply, depending on the position, the formation and the tactical role of the player. For example, high level performing players complete approximately 150-200 explosive energy actions during a game which implies a high participation of both the ATP/CP System and the Lactic Acid System. This is also verified clinically, since the levels of phosphocreatine and muscle pH are low while the levels of lactic acid, muscle lactic acid and adenosine monophosphate (metabolites in conditions of high anaerobic activity) are often in high levels in the blood stream and above the level of rest (Bangsbo et al., 2007). The accumulation of these metabolites has been found to be the cause for the state of exhaustion observed at the end of a game. It has been established that both the total distance covered as well as the total distance covered in high intensity are temporarily lower following periods of intense physical activity or towards the end of a game (Carling, 2013). This decrease in the parameters of physical performance is accompanied by a decrease in contacts with the ball (Rampinini et al., 2009) but not in the player's technical abilities (Rampinini et., 2009; Carling et al., 2011). However, it is important to note that when comparing the distance covered in the first and second halftime, the difference is approximately ~200±100m, something which has led some researchers to question whether the decrease in physical performance is a sign of fatigue during the game (Carling, 2013).

Technical abilities

Is fulfilling physical requirements all that is necessary in order to get the performance results that we intended? Let's not forget the four pillars of performance and move onto the analysis of the rest of the pieces that complete the players' performance puzzle.

Players do not simply run back and forth in the field. They also perform a collection of actions (with technical or physical dexterity), which will determine the result of a game (Barnes et al., 2014; Bush et al., 2015). There are differences depending on the position of the player and the table below presents some examples.

Performance

Positions	Tackling	Heading	Controlling the ball	Total touches with ball	Turn overs	Jumps
Wide Defenders	13,2	8	28,4	50,6	60,0	7,3
(v = 5)	3,0	1,7	11,1	13,2	6,5	3,3
Central defenders	14,4	13,4	23,4	53,4	52,8	11,8
(v = 5)	2,1	6,8	4,8	4,7	17,3	6,3
Midfielders	13,0	5,2	27,6	48,2	44,3	5,0
(α = 5)	8,5	3,1	20,9	19,0	9,1	4,4
Forwards/Strikers	11,6	13,0	25,0	53,2	42,3	13,3
(N = 5)	6,5	6,0	9,1	5,7	11,7	7,3
Total	13,1	9,9	26,1	51,4	49,9	9,4
(n = 20)	5,3	5,7	12,0	11,4	11,4	6,5

Soccer today, requires a very high skill level of these specific abilities and depending on the position played, some of these abilities become a reference point for the scouters of the teams. These technical abilities can be divided into actions with and without the ball. The goal of technical training is to achieve the best execution of an action while keeping the subject at the center of out training because the results are based on the athlete's personal technique. If for example, a player executes a skillful kickoff but does so with a personal style that does not follow the exact form of this move based on recent bibliography, then we must not try to change the way that the athlete executes this skill because he has accomplished the desired result.

Factors that affect Technical Abilities
The central nervous system (muscle and nerve collaboration)
Mental and psychological factors (perception, will etc.)
Anatomical factors (bone structure, muscle tone)
Physical factors (strength, speed, etc.)
Environmental factors
Personal development (receptiveness)

What makes a player stand out at the highest level is his developed perceptive abilities as well the precision with which he executes technical skills under pressure of space and time. Technical skill learning starts at a young age, and the young athlete is taught to develop and perfect his motor skills progressively and to allow reality to be the objective judge of his technical characteristics.

As Shea & Wulf (2005) have supported, stability may be an important factor when trying to obtain kinetic energy. Perhaps the variable training method of the parameters and the order in which these parameters are trained (random and grouped method of training) could have negative affects when trying to acquire skills.

In order to acquire skills that require moving the entire body, the variable training method was less beneficial for young children and beginners because beginners need to first discover the complex ways that allow kinematic control of all the separate parts of their body (Zipp & Gentile, 2010).

The base of the learning curve lies on the Constant Training Method, where the athlete is required to execute a specific skill without changing its parameters (speed of the ball, direction, speed of execution etc.).

Image 8: *Learning curve.*

Performance

For example, when learning how to make a short pass using the inside surface of the foot, (image 9) we place two players across one another at a distance of 10m. They repeat the exercise 10 times, during which we must explain the details for a correct execution of the skill (positioning of the support leg, trajectory of the kicking foot, what part of the foot makes contact with the ball, correct positioning of the arms and torso etc.).

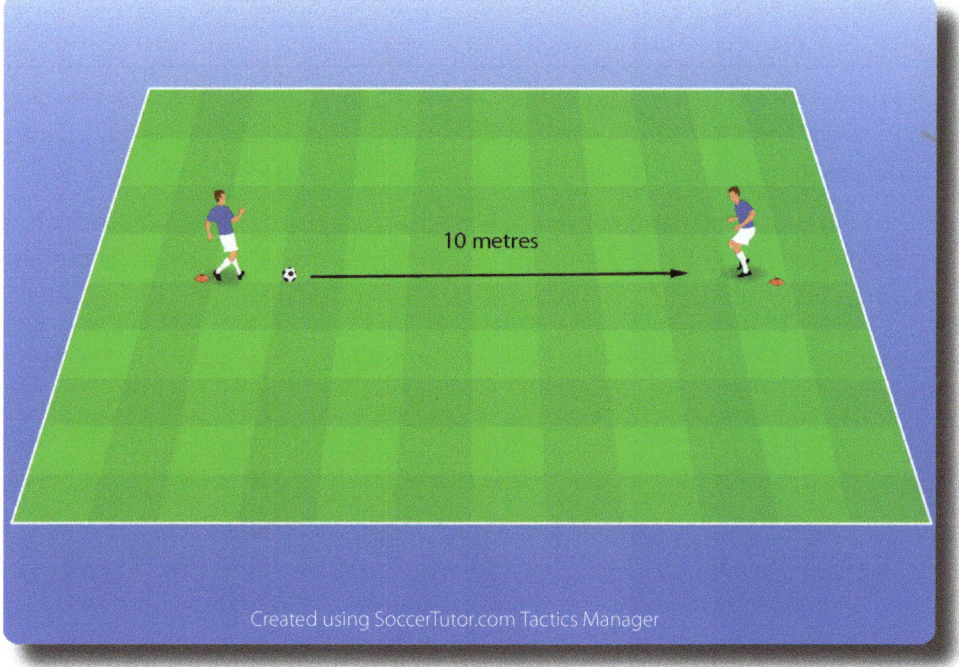

Image 9: *Passing.*

These are the types of exercises that we will be using while executing our Periodization Training Model as a way to remind the central nervous system of some basic skills and as an opportunity to teach using simple observations during training. When dealing with adult athletes, it is very difficult to change a kinematic model even if we observe faulty patterns, especially during the in-season period. Their kinematic model is imprinted in their brain, so if we want to make any adjustment, it needs to be done with high volume of training and not while the athlete is preparing for a game. As soon as the athlete feels pressure his brain will revert to the kinematic model that has been imprinted since his childhood.

Another case in which we use the Constant Training Method is when we want to change the way a skill is executed. But can we improve the established technique even to a small degree? How many times have we heard that the outcome of the game was in the details? The improvement of even these small details can determine both the outcome of a game and the future of a player.

When using a Constant Training Method, with steady parameters of execution, the duration is short, the intensity is low and we provide the athlete a break after each completion, it can be used as an activation/warm up or as an introduction into the main training section.

Image 10 presents a drill where the player drives the ball between the cones either with his left or right foot (or using both) and he then shoots the ball towards the goal using the inside of his foot.

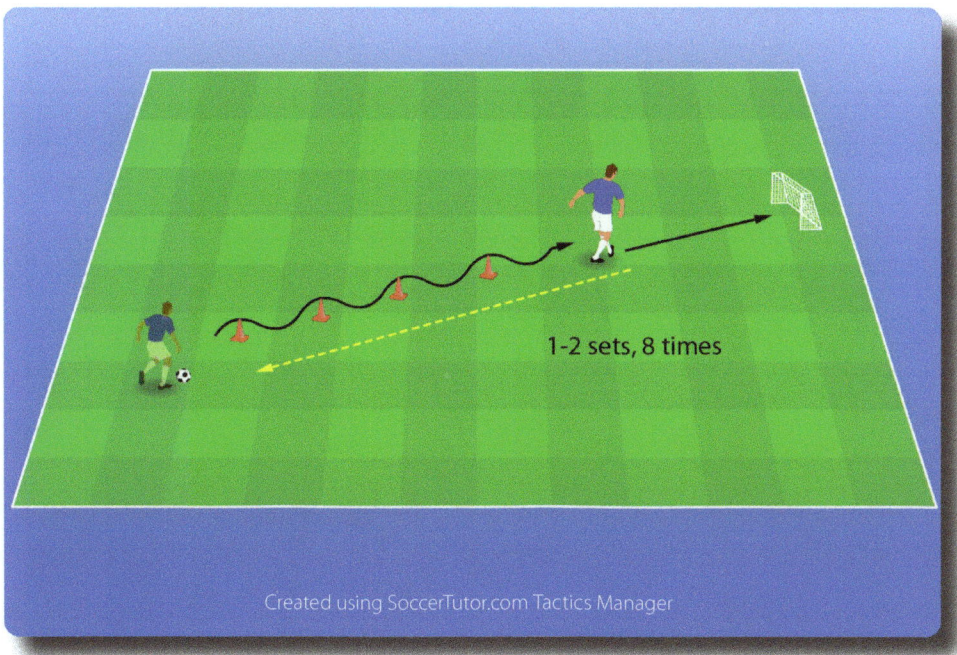

Image 10: *Driving the ball.*

Performance

Once the athlete has learned how to properly execute a skill, we then add some parameters that will help him exercise his skill under conditions that simulate game scenarios. The use of the variable training method, as mentioned extensively in bibliography (Kadzin, 1975, Shute & Gawlick, 1995), helps the athlete to not rely on actions that will limit and generalize the range of his skills. For example, when training in receiving the ball, it is important to have variable parameters which lead to a variable training method, since rarely will a ball be thrown with the same speed and at the same height during a game. The more realistic the training is, the more pressure is placed on the athlete to perform during the execution of these exercises in order to accomplish the goals. As in the case of executing a passing drill, we must make sure that the ball is received from different angles and at variable speeds (image 11). In this exercise the athlete completes a pass-pass back and sideways- pass forward and a final pass between the poles. The ball receiver must drive the ball swiftly. The players interchange positions at each station.

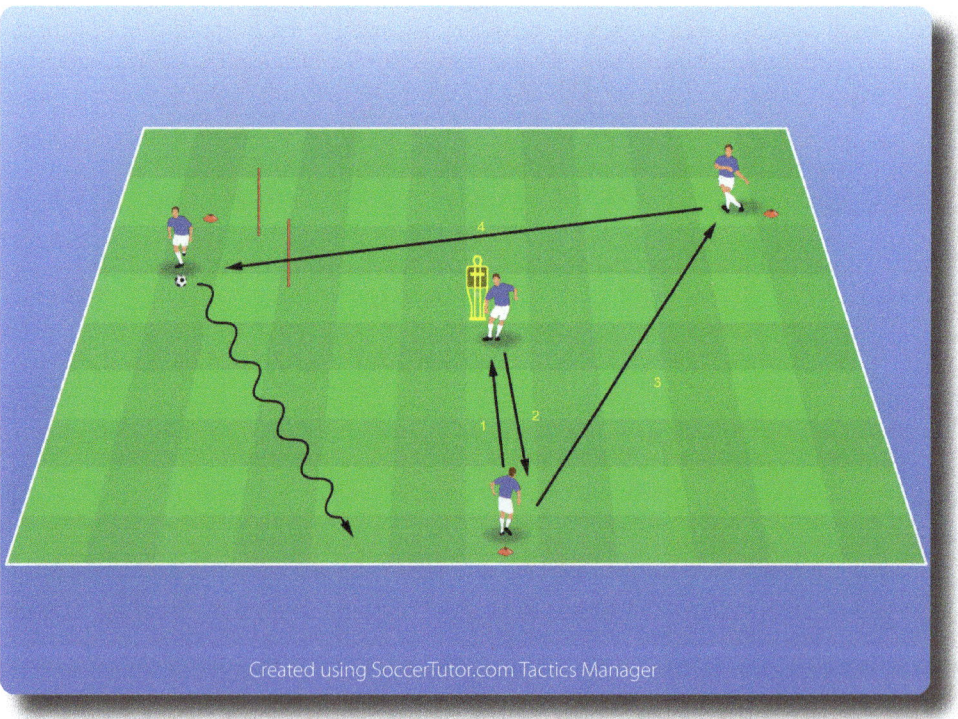

Image 11: *Passing drill.*

This constant variability forces the athlete to perfect the execution of the specific skill by simulating the conditions that he will face within a game. The player is forced to constantly change his kinematic model by giving new orders to his muscles through his neurons. The muscles will then send this information to his joints in order to succeed in accomplishing the anticipated result.

This form of training is vastly used in soccer today at all levels, as it can be used either as preparation for the main training section for the improvement of skills (pass, receive, heading, drive, shot, etc.) as well as in the case of shadow games which allow formations to develop in the whole field (e.g. 11 v 11 formation) without having the pressure of an opponent.

The image below presents an example of tactical training with the variable method. In this exercise, the ball moves moves progressively from the goal to the opponent area in order to score.

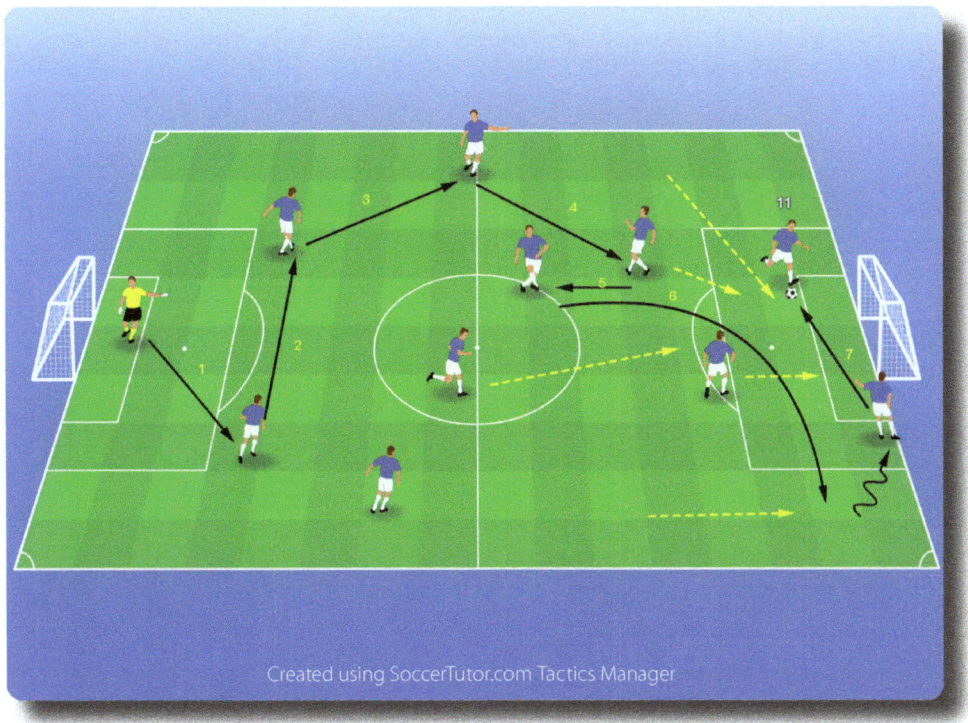

Image 12: *Tactics training.*

Performance

The final stage of technique training in our periodized training model contains within it the element of chance. When an athlete has completed all levels of training, possesses the technical skills that the sport requires and has reached a professional level of practice, only the random method of training can help him improve even further. During this method of training, realistic parameters are introduced into the training regiment and the player is now required to execute the skills he is in the process of training, under the pressure of time, space and an opponent. In the case of an exercise in ball possession, where the player is asked to pass the ball between cones, various skills need to be executed in random order (pass, receive, moving without the ball etc.) and in random form (angle of ball reception, strength, speed, etc.) This randomness perfects his acquired skills while training under circumstances that simulate the conditions he will encounter during a game (image 13).

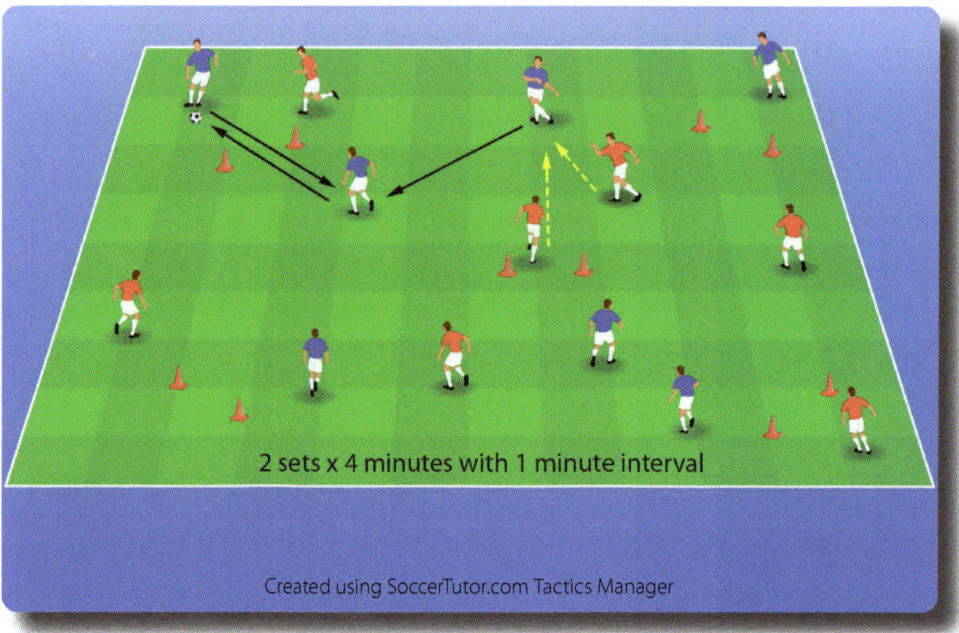

Image 13: *Ball possession drill.*

In almost all competitive games, players train their technical abilities to the greatest and most realistic degree.

Have you ever wondered when a forward trains under the most realistic circumstances in the skills required for finishing? In an exercise with finishing in which he will receive a pass and shoot undisturbed, or in a game 5 v 5 with two goalkeepers and the pressure of the opponents, exhaustion, the angle of the body, reaction etc?

Depending on the number of associations, the load during technical training varies depending on the number of contacts with the ball or the amount of specialized skills that need to be executed. We need to take this under consideration if we want to know the real training load each training model bears. (Image 14).

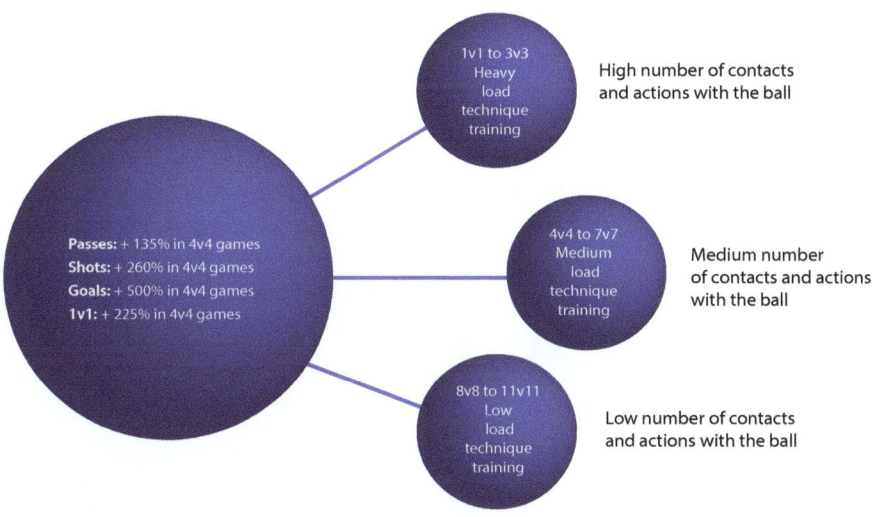

Image 14: *Technical training and small-sided games.*

Therefore, if we want to select a game that will improve the skill of ball possession we will see that by choosing a 10 v 10 game and observing one player in this game, there will be specific actions (kinematic skills) with and without the ball. If we then change the number of players in the game to 5 v 5 we will immediately observe a raise in the number of these actions, which will result in a rise of the intensity and subsequently of the training load at this specific technique.

Performance

When designing our periodized training, the order with which we implement the various training methods (constant/variable/random) depends on the needs, abilities and demands of our players. It is our responsibility as trainers to not only create and apply good and stimulating training regiments but also to understand the true needs of our players and apply the appropriate stimuli that will improve and stabilize their performance.

Analyzing the technical abilities of our players, requires focusing on the repetition of technical actions during all 4 phases of the game on a personal level (image). In order to determine the level of their technical abilities we observe the percentage of their skills successfully executed, or the way in which they were executed during training sessions or games. These technical skills must be carefully monitored and evaluated during training and official games.

The execution of these skills must be under the most realistic of circumstances and under the pressure of time and space and not by simply performing various technical ability evaluation drills.

The evaluation tests that are available in the market are helpful for us to create a kinematic profile of the player but cannot help us evaluate whether a play-

Technical Characteristics
Corner kicks
Driving the ball
Dribbling
Finishing
1st Touch
Free kicks
Heading
Long shots
Long pass
Defending/Marking
Pass
Penalty shot
Tackling
Motor skills

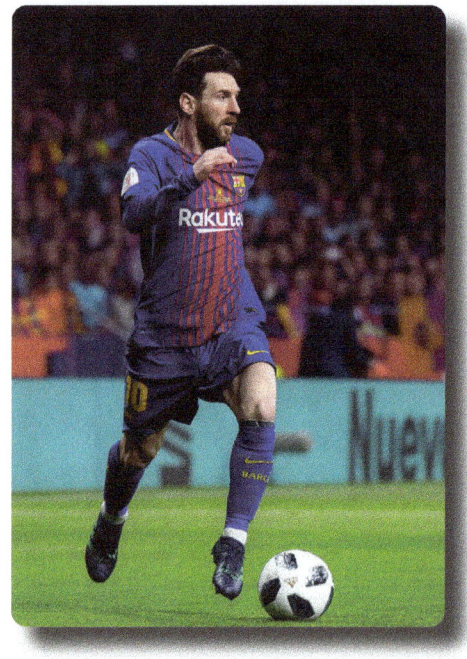

er can successfully execute those skills during a game because the demands of an official game are considerably higher than the demands of an evaluation test. What we know for sure is that Technical abilities play an equally important role when trying to reach efficiency in soccer today.

Tactical abilities

In the following scene we see an example of a choice that Almeida, a player for the national team of Portugal, could have made while trying to score a goal during a game against the national team of Spain. Despite they are 3 vs 3, Almeida takes an unsuccessful shot 30m away from goal instead of passing to Nani who could have then made a pass to Ronaldo who was outside the box.

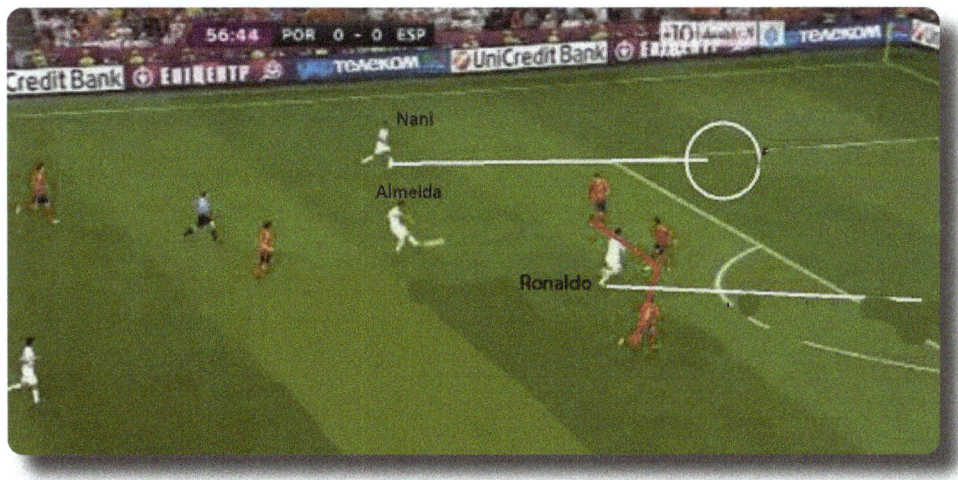

Performance

These are the kinds of tactical actions that players are constantly challenged to make during the course of a game in order to realize the particular objective of their team.

Whether they are defending or attacking and whether they are in possession of the ball or not, the tactical behavior of a team is usually determined through video analysis, during which the coach, the analyst, the scouter etc. will focus on the actions of the players during the four phases of the game on a individual, sub-group and group level (image 15).

Image 15: *Player actions during the 4 phases of a game.*

Strong and weak points of both our team and the opponent team are analyzed which results in applying specialized tactics during the microcycle of the game.

General Tactics = general tactical principles we want our team to follow.
Specialized Tactics = specialized tactical instructions in relation to the opponent

The coach is responsible for training in order to cultivate tactical abilities in his players. The role of the physical trainer during these sessions is limited to advising about the physical consequences that this training will have on the players (impact of the imposed training load). Coaches today have varied methods of how they choose to tactically prepare during the weekly training plan. Some choose to offer guidance and advise to their players during an 11 vs 11 game while supplying many breaks for commentary and making changes, placing the players with a low tempo and low intensity. Others use games of medium to high intensity, where the players must find solutions that will help them in the upcoming game. The physical trainer is called upon to fill in the gaps that are created during these training sessions and help the players reach their highest competitive performance potential.

Cognitive and psychological abilities

Perhaps the most difficult characteristics to analyze are those of the Mental and Psychological abilities of the players since it requires time to observe them as well as the way that these abilities interact with the other 3 categories (Technical Development, Tactical Development, Physical Development). In order to determine the level of each mental and psychological component it not only requires time with the players themselves but also with their team-mates and occasionally with sports psychologists.

Many scouters have the habit of observing and documenting the types of reactions that players display during the course of a game, mainly in relation to their mental abilities. The table below presents an example that lists some characteristics.

Athlete's mental condition
Creativity
Predictability
Perception
Composure
Aggression
Concentration
Decisiveness

In order to complete the athlete's profile, a similar chart could be filled out from a specialist (i.e. sports psychologist) containing information about their psychological abilities. The table below lists some characteristics.

Performance

Athlete's Psychological condition
Level of self-esteem
Handling of senses
Trust in one self
Goals
Quality of inner dialogue
Motives
Learning and concentration
Ability to overcome victory, loss and injuries

It is very important for us to know how the athlete receives and reacts to various stimuli. These can be as simple as how he reacts to being reprimanded during training or if he change his behaviors to the team after scoring a critical goal.

The effect that his mental condition has on his overall presence as well as the way that he interacts with his team-mates, along with observing and urging his improvement will help us complete the puzzle of the 4 pillars of performance.

Synopsis

By determining the needs of the player during the course of a game we can design the training process that will improve their weaknesses and maintain their performance at the highest possible level and for the maximum possible period of time.

A key point for our understanding of the Periodization Training Model is the motto "we train like we play" that we have seen printed as a logo on a number of team t-shirts or training center billboards. What this motto means is not that we will run 12.000 m or work at a 70-95% capacity of our maximum heart rate for 90 minutes during each training session. Nor that our concentration will be unwavering from the first to the last minute of our training as it is during an official game.

What this phrase means is that through the training process we will set on the principles that we want for our team to follow in official games, with the least possible diversion.

In a sense, training gains a ritualistic significance where the dedication with which we adhere to the plan that has been decided, also reflects the success to come.

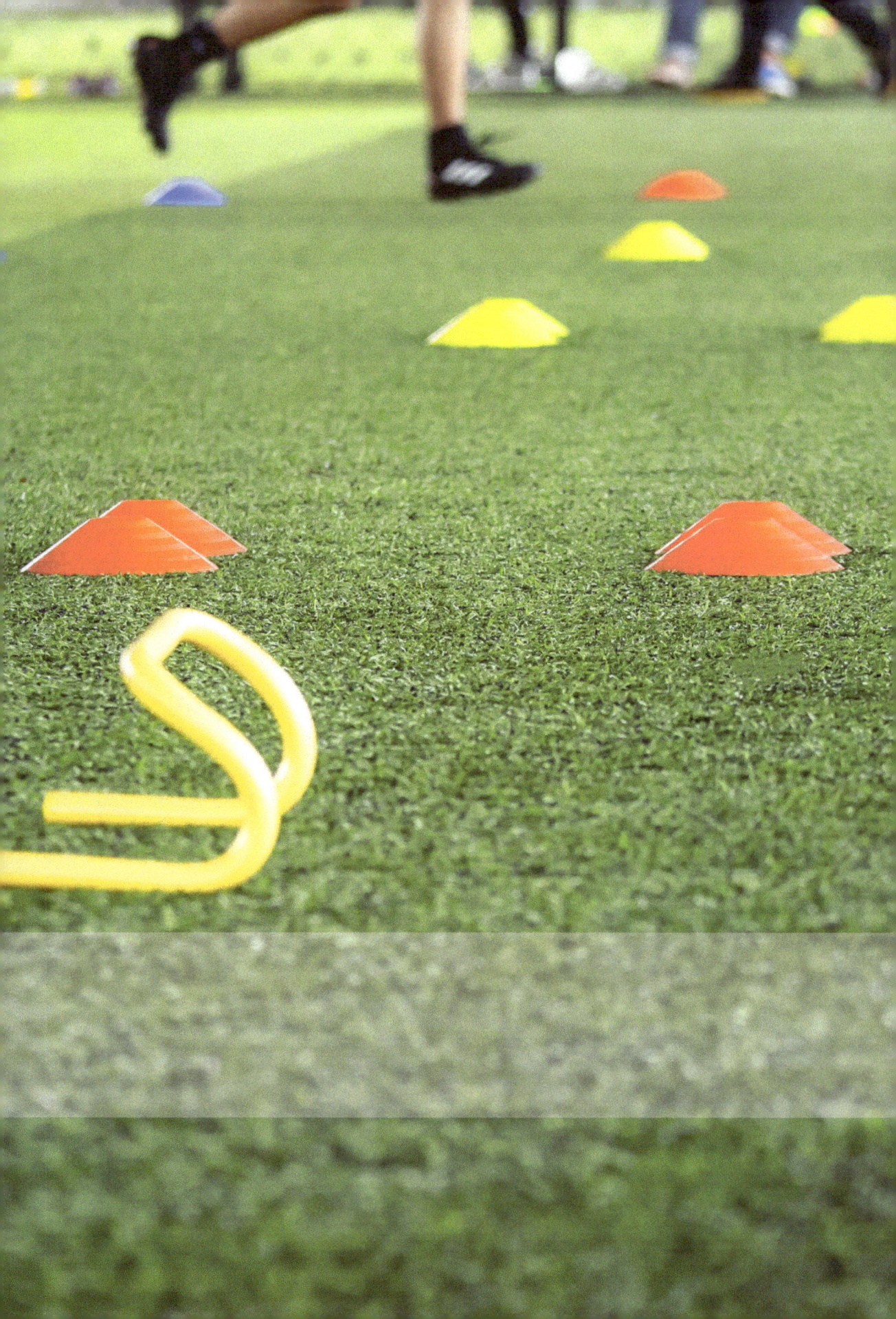

season

Season

An annual season is broken down into 3 periods
- Transition period
- Preperation Period
- Competitive Period

The purpose of the Transition Period is the deliberate and controlled decrease of performance and the recovery of the players, the purpose of the Preparation Period is to maximize performance to the desired levels and the purpose of the Competitive Period is to maintain or even to increase its specific elements (Turner & Stewart, 2014), (see image below).

FITNESS TRAINING PROGRAM FOR F.C. ASTERAS TRIPOLIS

MONTH	JUNE	JULY	AUGUST		SEPTEMBER-MAY
Periodization	Transition	General Preparation	Specialised Preparation	Tapering Phase	Regular season
Endurance	Cross training, active rehabilitation, general endurance	General - Specific Endurance	Specific Endurance	Specific Endurance	Games - Specific Endurance
Strength	Maintaining/increasing strength levels	Anatomical adaptations	Maximum Strength	Power	Maintaining strength levels
Speed		Preparative period	Spesific speed, Speed endurance, Agility	Spesific speed, Reaction speed, Agility	Maintaining speed levels
Physical Fitness Tests		(1)			(2) September (3) January (4) May

s11.gr

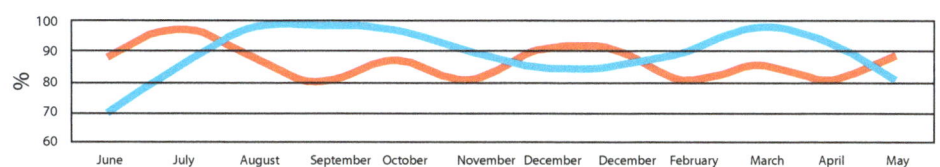

Image 16: *Training intensity and volume graph. Intensity=Blue / Volume= Red.*

Transition Period

The Transition Period may differ depending on the amount of time that the players have from the end of their obligations towards their team until the new season begins. As we mentioned earlier, the goal of this period is the deliberate decrease of the players' performance as well as their recuperation, but under close control and minimal fluctuation. Depending on the level of their participation during the competitive period, their needs for improvement, and the injuries they may have sustained during the season, it is crucial that the players follow an organised and systematic training method during the Transition Period. Many European clubs try to bring their players to a good level at the beginning of the Preparation Period by having them partake in rigorous training programs during the Transition Period. Below you can see a general example of a 6 week Transition Period training plan.

	Monday	Tuesday	Wednesday	Thursday	Friday	Saturday	Sunday
Week 1							
Week 2							
Week 3	Strength & Endurance		Strength		Strength & Endurance		
Week 4	Strength & Endurance		Endurance		Strength & Endurance		
Week 5	Strength & Endurance		Strength & Endurance		Strength & Endurance		
Week 6	Strength & Endurance		Strength & Endurance		Endurance		

Season

Typical strength training workout during the Transition Period: 6-12 total body exercises either with external resistance or with the use of body weight. Complete 2-3 sets x 8-12 repetitions.

Illustrations of typical exercises:

Typical endurance training workout during the Transition Period: 3 repetitions x 8'-10' running at 75-85% M.H.R. or 2 x 6' running alternating jogging with strides across the sidelines of the field.

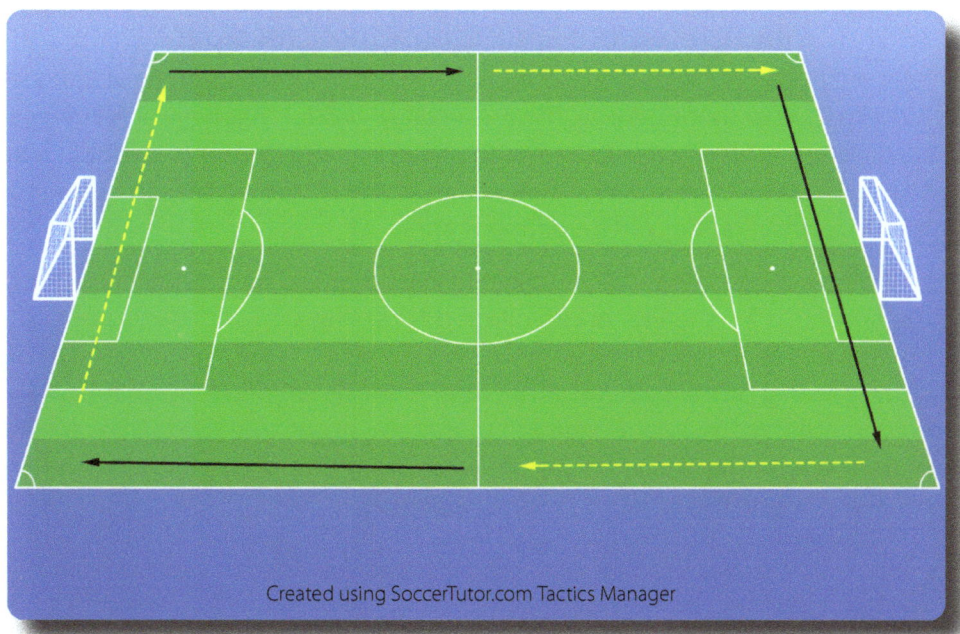

Image 17: *Exercise for endurance training.*

The following table includes directives from UEFA:

TRANSITION PERIOD	
Duration	4-6 weeks (two sub-periods)
Goal	**Deliberate recuperation after the completion of the competitive period** • Active and passive recovery (physical, emotional, mental) - revitalisation
Contents	Relaxed running for 30', gymnastics, group sports, swimming etc.
Training Load	During the Transition period, the level of intensity is low to average

Season

Preparation Period

Because the Preparation Period is in the beginning, it is also a very crucial period since as they say "well begun is half done". From the first day that the athletes are present in the team, the training on our principles and the abilities we want to give to them begins. The preparation model that we will follow may be different regarding to its training process because teams with obligations to international competitions, that have shorter transition seasons as well as high level players, may have a different approach.

This is a chapter that we will cover in brief though, since the philosophy of the approach for the Preparation Period is usually similar. It begins with the general and ends with the specific during the whole spectrum of the 4 pillars of the training process (technical, tactical, physical, cognitive/psycological abilites) in order to create the foundation that the player and the team will build onto through time. Based on the UEFA coaching program, a Preperation Period must include the following specific points:

	PREPARATION PERIOD (basic points)
Duration	6-8 weeks
Goal	**Performance Improvement** • Physical fitness • Technical and tactical behavior • Training of a basic formation • Psychological I factors • Cultivating team spirit
Contents	• We move from general to specialised preparation • Maintain the principle of progression
Load Intensity	• The intensity begins at a low level and progressively increases to a high level as we grow closer to the Regular season • The high level of of volume, will decrease and stabilise as we enter the regular season.

Periodization Training Method - Maximizing Performance in Soccer

Competitive Period

The periodization model presented and analysed in this book refers to the Competitive Period, which is also the period of "judgement" for the entire team staff. Usually the one who wins is the one who has done everything right. I would like to differentiate my personal position by daring to say that it is the time when performance exceeds the result, at least for those of us who know the sport. Also, let us not oversee the fact that participating in a championship is a marathon and in a marathon what matters is not how you start it but how you finish it!

During the Competitive Period, the coaching staff begins the design of the teams training in order to better determine the training loads and to monitor the goals that they have set. A daily training regimen is set each day and in the beginning of the week they design the training schedule until the next game and each month they plan in order to stay in line with the coaching philosophy.

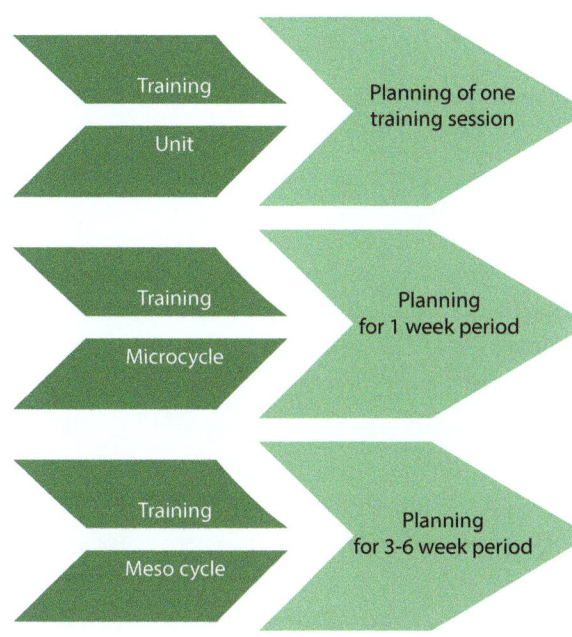

Image 18: *The base for training planning.*

Season

The periodization model that will be presented here, sets the foundations for constant improvement throughout the Competitive Period. Therefore it functions more as a plan for performance improvement rather than a plan for performance maintenance during the Competitive Period.

The periodization model that I will analyse can be broken down into 3 main weekly training blocks plus 2 optional blocks. Each one in its turn plays a specific role but also during the sequence of the next block in terms of the training during the Competitive Period. The order of the three main blocks is the following:

1. Endurance Block
2. Strength Block
3. Speed Block

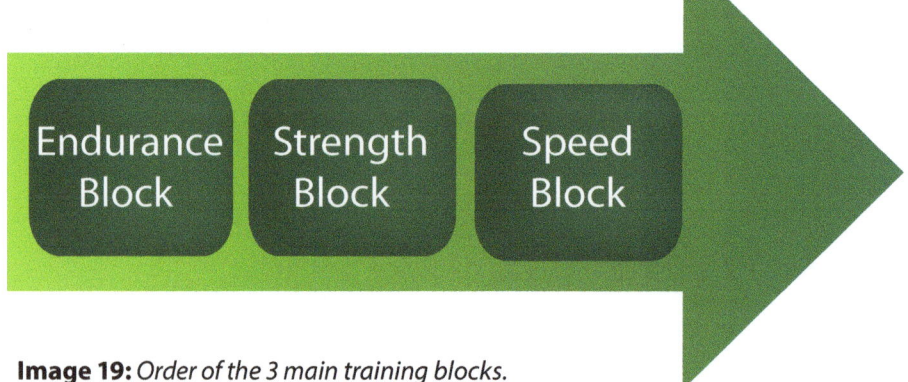

Image 19: *Order of the 3 main training blocks.*

The logical training sequence for coaches following a specific model with an organised approach to the training process allows opportunities for interventions and changes in a controlled and simple manner, even if those changes mean that we are diverging from our initial ideas (Gamble, 2006).

What is innovative about the training model that will be presented is the fact that it contains periods of increased emphasis on the basic skills (endurance, strength, speed) whenever the competitive program of the team allows for it. Within the weekly training cycle, this is accomplished by increasing the volume of training of a specific element (in order to make adaptations and improvements) whilst the other elements are preserved at the regular volume of training (for maintenance purpose). Therefore during each weekly microcycle, we will select and focus on one element which will be our focus for 2 days during that week while all the other elements will be the focus of training for 1 day of the weekly microcycle. It is important that the focus changes from one weekly cycle to another, in order to make sure that we have focused on every element when the mesocycle has been completed. Therefore, within the endurance block we select and focus on the element of endurance by providing endurance training for 2 training units within the weekly microcycle. The same stands for the strength and speed block, where once again and depending on the week, we will select and focus on 2 stimulations (endurance, speed or strength) per each training microcycle. Following the completion of three weekly microcycles, 2 weekly microcycles of maintenance and recovery can follow, depending on the workload of your players and the teams schedule (e.g. Cup games, signs of fatigue etc.). This is how we create a 5 week mesocycle that contains intense training for maximising performance as well as gradual recovery for the re-initiation of the cycle.

1. Endurance Block
2. Strength Block
3. Speed Block
4. Maintenance Block
5. Recovery Block

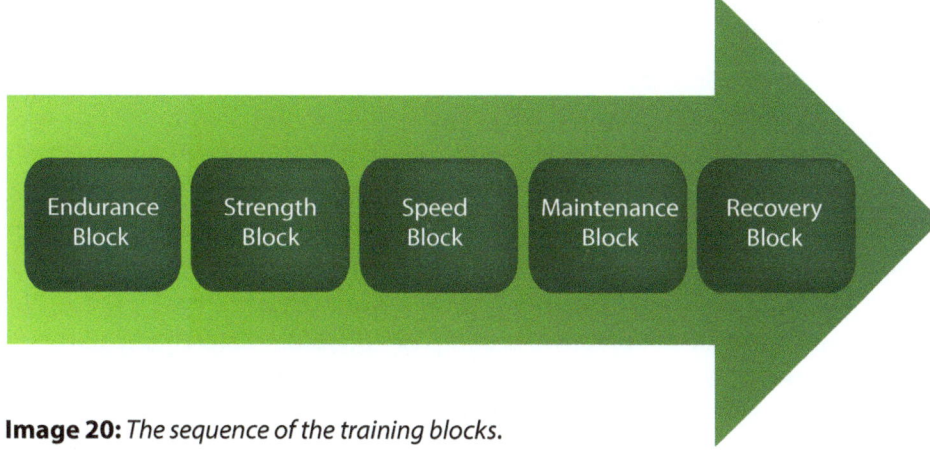

Image 20: *The sequence of the training blocks.*

Season

A Maintenance Block within our periodization model is considered a weekly micro-cycle with an emphasis on training endurance, strength and speed once a week. The aim of the Maintenance Block, is to maintain the physical abilities of the players without additional emphasis (Van Winckel et al., 2014). It is the typical micro-cycle designed to maintain the abilities of your players.

The Recovery Block is a weekly micro-cycle that has no emphasis on the physical characteristics of the players. During the Recovery Block there are no training units devoted to strength and speed, with the exception of 1-2 sets of reaction speed drills the day before a game. The training units that provide some degree of endurance stimulus are only those of general or specific tactical training that the coach will use during the week. The main function in using such micro-cycles is to deload the athletes from stressful situations and revitalise them for the course of the championship. The table below presents an example of a Recovery Block.

Sunday	Monday	Tuesday	Wednesday	Thursday	Friday	Saturday
Game	Day Off	Rehabilitation				Activation
			Technical	Technical	Technical	Technical
			Tactical	Tactical	Tactical	Tactical
			Stress Management	Stress Management	Stress Management	Stress Management

When the calendar of the official games is known, the coach will begin a thorough planning. In some leagues the seasonal schedule is presented in 2 rounds, therefore make a note of the official games of the first round (but only those with one game per micro-cycle) and note down the first free 3-weeks block (3 sequential microcycles with 1 game/microcycle). During the first week of this 3 week block, place the periodized sequence of 2 training units with the Endurance Block, during the second week place the Strength Block and during the third week place the Speed Block. If there is a 4th or 5th week with one per micro-cycle, place the Maintenance Block and the Recovery Block accordingly while taking under consideration signs that your players may be presenting (i.e. fatigue, levels of performance accomplished, accumulated game participation time). Alternatively you could also repeat the 3 week cycle with the sequential Endurance, Strength and Speed blocks.

The logic behind this specific periodization model is based on the constant interaction with the signs that the team displays, since placing overload blocks (i.e. weekly training microcycles containing 2 training units in one of the three abilities) certainly adds to the training load. With every 3 blocks that you complete, it is important to evaluate the effect that they have had on the performance of the players and make a judgement call as to whether you will repeat the 3 blocks or whether you will add a maintenance block or a recovery block instead. Your daily interaction with the players as well as the levels of standard you have set for their performance, should be your guide when choosing whether you will repeat the 3 blocks (Endurance Block-Strength Block-Speed Block) or whether you will implement Maintenance or Recovery Block. This process will contunue until the Competitive Period has been completed.

During microcycles that have 2 games (i.e. championship game or cup game) if 70% of the players play both games, you can consider them participation as an Endurance Block and therefore you can continue with a Strength block and a Speed block. If the coach chooses to rotate the players in the 2 out of the 3 consecutive games, then the microcycle can be characterized depending on the content of the training for the "starting" players within the microcycle, (emphasis on endurance, strength or speed) as an Endurance-Strength-Speed-Maintenance or Recovery Block. Below you can see an example for the 8 first games of the regular season.

Regular Season	Training Block
Week 1	Endurance Block
Week 2	Strength block
Week 3	Speed Block
Week 4	Maintenance Block
Week 5	Recovery Block
Week 6	Endurance Block
Week 7	Strength Block
Week 8	Speed Block

At this point it is important to remember that the aim of our periodization model (Endurance Block –Strength Block-Speed Block) is to improve your players' performance. In the case you believe that they have reached the desired results in their performance, then you can implement typical maintenance and recovery microcycles (containing 1 training unit per ability per week) for a large period of time or even for the rest of the season (Papadakis et.,al 2015).

Season

Our sequential overloading periodization model is based on the theory that "we train when we can" which means: whenever the athletes' competitive schedule and potential allow us, (we) train them. During the time when competitive schedule is too tight, the body and the mind of the players are already under pressure. If we want to improve their characteristics in time, we must plan their training on a yearly basis in order to maximise their performance.

The performance threshold is different for each player and for each team separately and minimal differences (regardless if they are more or less) in each 4 areas of performance can determine the overall performance of the players. In order for the team to function properly overall, we must be very careful in selecting the training model that we will use. This requires of course meticulous observation of the training and careful judgement by the coach in relation to the performance of his players during training and official games.

"Breaking down" the system

Imagine a mesocycle containing 3 micro-cycles (weekly periods) in which the contents of training for gradual improvement are placed in such a way, that we do not under-train (the phenomenon in which the quantity, quality and sequence of training stimulation, is not adequate for maintaining or improving skills) nor over-train (the phenomenon in which the quantity, quality and sequence of training stimulation, is too excessive for maintaining or improving skills), (Chad, 2010; Van Winckel et., al 2014). The image below presents two examples of the training sequence.

We must not overlook players who have a lower level of participation in the official games, or none at all, and therefore need higher training load in order to maintain or improve their 4 areas of performance (Yule, 2014). These players are always a challenge for the coaching staff and must always be treated as equals in relation to the other members of the squad.

A periodization model that was used from a soccer club in the Greek Superleague is a good example on how to deal with the uneven distribution of training loads amongst regular starters and bench players during the competitive period. The Superleague club used a sequential overloading training model per micro-cycle and succeeded in attaining a top 1/3 table position

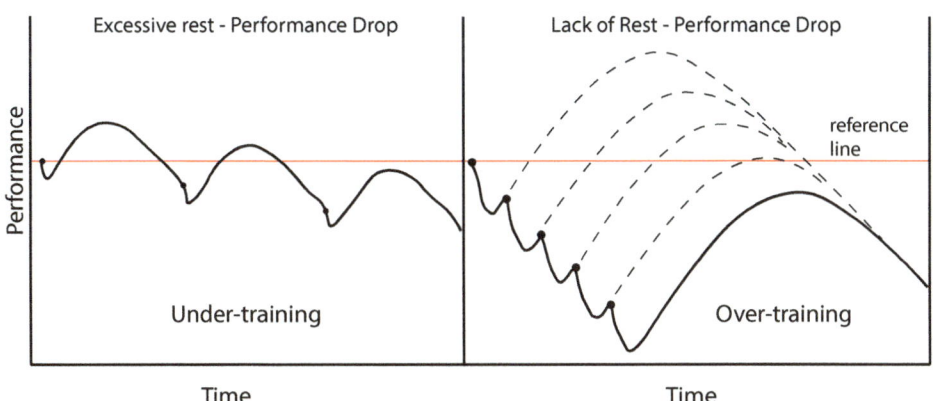
Image 21: *Performance decrease due to under-training or over-training.*

earning qualification for European competition, even though they mainly used players with minimal experience in the Premier Super League and were not allowed to make any player transfers due to penalty issues from the federation. The analysis of the yearly training plan, as well as the training contents, was published in the Journal of Australian Strength and Conditioning, one of the best peer-reviewed scientific journals in the field of strength and conditioning globally (Papadakis et al., 2015).

The logic of player handling was based on the concept of subjecting the players to a training stimulation of the same ability twice during a micro-cycle. The player is called upon to complete training in Endurance or Strength or Speed two times in the same week but with a lighter training for the second training day (te day that is closer to the upcoming game).. In order to not jeopardise the players participation (with fatigue induced injury) the days closer to the game we will use the same stimulation but with tightly controlled training loads while trying to observe with precision, the consequences the particular stimulation will have on the athlete.

In this model, the three weeks (plus the two optional weeks) of our initial periodization model follows the following sequence:

- Endurance Block (2 training units for endurane, 1 training unit for strength, 1 training unit for speed)
- Strength Block (2 training units for strength, 1 training unit for endurance, 1 training unit for speed)
- Speed Block (2 training units for speed, 1 training unit for endurance, 1 training unit for strength)

Season

And depending on the annual official game engagements and your planning:
- Maintenance (1 training unit for each endurance-strength-speed)
- Recovery (no emphasis on physical abilities)

A complete plan of our periodization model, for players of all categories and skill levels, is analysed in the following tables. The particular plan concerns clubs and coaching staffs that have selected the second day after the official game of their team as their day-off. In this case, players who participated for less that 45 minutes will follow a high intensity and medium duration training session the day following the game, whilst all players will participate in the training plan presented from the third day after a game and on-ward, the physical fitness coach can collaborate with the rest of the team specialists and create additional contents for technical/tactical traning as well as physical fitness for those players who are in need of additional training. For example, a wide defender who did not participate in the last game, can remain in the training field after training and practice on crossing, or a central defender can attend the gym for additional training in strength.

Tables containing the Endurance Block, Strength Block, Speed Block, Maintenance Block, Recovery Block follow on pages 52 to 55.

Season

Endurance Block

Day	Sunday	Monday	Tuesday	Wednesday
morning		*Group A* (those who played > 45 min. on Sunday): **Recovery** *Group B* (those who played < 45 min. on Sunday): **Endurance (medium-high load)**	REST *	Technical/Tactical *Endurance (medium/high load)*
afternoon	GAME		REST	Strength (medium/high load)

* *The resting day of the team can be reversed*

Strength Block

Day	Sunday	Monday	Tuesday	Wednesday
morning		*Group A* (those who played > 45 min. on Sunday): **Recovery** *Group B* (those who played < 45 min. on Sunday): **Endurance (medium-high load)**	REST *	Technical/Tactical *Endurance (medium/high load)*
afternoon	GAME		REST	**Strength (medium/high load)**

* *The resting day of the team can be reversed*

Speed Block

Day	Sunday	Monday	Tuesday	Wednesday
morning		*Group A* (those who played > 45 min. on Sunday): **Recovery** *Group B* (those who played < 45 min. on Sunday): **Endurance (medium-high load)**	REST *	**Speed (acceleration, medium/high load)** Technical/Tactical Endurance (medium/high load)
afternoon	GAME		REST	Strength (medium/high load)

* *The resting day of the team can be reversed*

season

Endurance Block

Day	Thursday	Friday	Saturday	Sunday
morning	Technical/Tactical	Technical/Tactical ***Endurance (low load)***	Speed (reaction, low load) Technical/Tactical	
afternoon				GAME

Strength Block

Day	Thursday	Friday	Saturday	Sunday
morning	Technical/Tactical	***Strength (reactive, low load)*** Technical/Tactical	Speed (reaction, low load) Technical/Tactical	
afternoon				GAME

Speed Block

Day	Thursday	Friday	Saturday	Sunday
morning	Technical/Tactical	***Speed (reaction, low load)*** Technical/Tactical	Technical/Tactical	
afternoon				GAME

B SEASON

Season

Maintenance Block

Day	Sunday	Monday	Tuesday	Wednesday
morning		**Group A** (those who played for Over 45 min. on Sunday): **Recovery** **Group B** (those who played less that 45 min. on Sunday): **Endurance (medium-high load)**	REST	Technique/Tactics Endurance (medium/high load)
		↔	*	
afternoon	GAME		REST	Strength (medium/high load)

* The resting day of the team can be reversed

Recovery Block

Day	Sunday	Monday	Tuesday	Wednesday
morning		**Group A** (those who played for Over 45 min. on Sunday): **Recovery** **Group B** (those who played less that 45 min. on Sunday): **Endurance (medium-high load)**	REST	Technique/Tactics
		↔	*	
afternoon	GAME		REST	

* The resting day of the team can be reversed

Periodization Training Method - Maximizing Performance in Soccer

Maintenance Block

Day	Thursday	Friday	Saturday	Sunday
morning	Technique/Tactics	Technique/Tactics	Speed (reaction, low load) Technique/Tactics	
afternoon				GAME

Recovery Block

Day	Thursday	Friday	Saturday	Sunday
morning	Technique/Tactics	Technique/Tactics	Speed (reaction, low load) Technique/Tactics	
afternoon				GAME

B SEASON

Season

Wave-like mathematical sequence

In order to continue discussing our periodization model of three weeks (plus two optional weeks) it is important to refer to the entire regular season. The entire plan is based on a "wave-like" mathematical sequence graph with a tendency to increase.

The three week plan not only follows a vertical sequence of differentiation, but also a horizontal one, since the constant application of the same stimulation brings performance to a plateau, stopping any tendency for improvement over time (image 22).

The sequence of the annual training interventions must be in a "wave-like", increasing form in order to give the players the necessary time and the opportunity to adjust and improve over time (see image below).

It is best to try to alternate the duration and intensity of the stimulation in such a way, that at the end of the season you will have raised the level of your players.

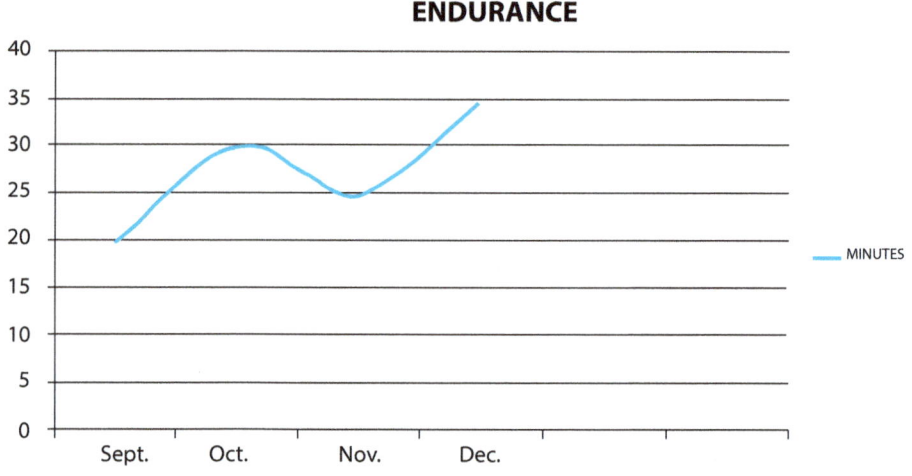

Image 22: *Mathematical sequence of endurance Graph.*

The goal of a training load is to disrupt the homeostasis of the organism. In the organism's effort to cope, it eventually improves in the analogous time. When the stimulation remains "easy" the body will not respond in a way that will result in its improvement and over time, performance will decrease. When the stimulation is repetitively "difficult", the body does not recover and this will not result in an improved performance and also can result in injury.

Applying the mathematical sequence, allows us alternating period of increased training stimuli with periods of decreased training stimuli in order to increase the possibilities of performance improvements over time (Van Winckel et.,al 2014; Gamble, 2006).

physical abilities

Physical abilities

Endurance

In regards to physical fitness and especially the area of endurance, we must pay careful attention to the internal and external training load that the athlete receives during training.

Internal load = the physiological and psychological stress induced by training
External load = the volume of actions that the player executed quantitatively
Subjective facts = facts that inform us of the physiological and psychological situation the athlete is in from the perspective of the athlete himself.
Objective facts = facts that inform us and can be measured either through observation or through tests.

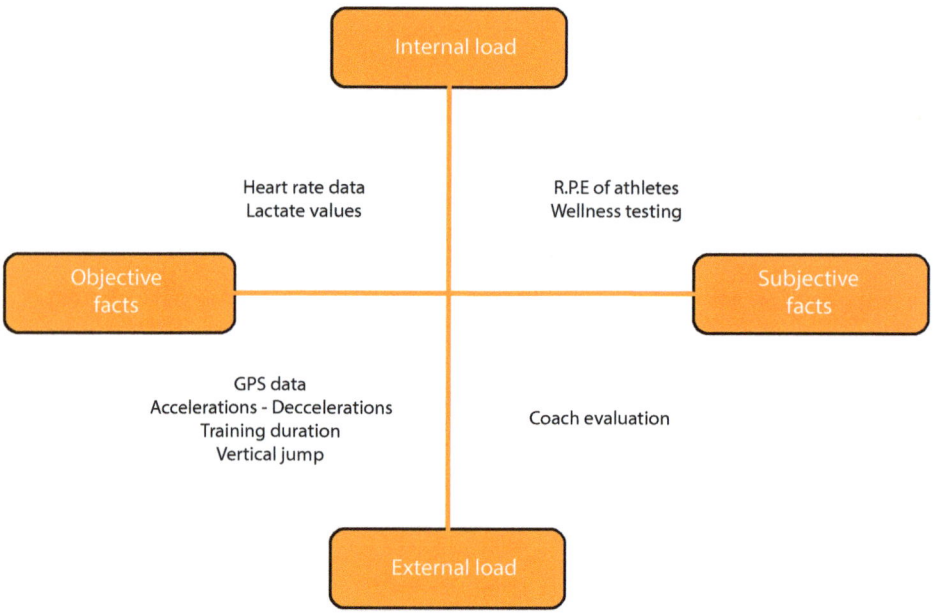

Image 23: *Physical fitness.*

The training result is a consequence of the external training load and the stress level that is induced for each player separately (internal load) (Virou & Virou, 2000). In soccer the external load tends to be similar amongst the players due to the fact that they train as a group, though this does not always result in the same internal load. What we conclude from this is that it is very important to quantify both the external and internal load in order to assess the training process (Morgans et al., 2014).

Many fitness coaches and sports scientists tried to evolve endurance training by making it more complex than running so they introduced the use of the ball and the execution of kinetic patterns that simulate the actions of a player during a game (Little, 2009; Little & Williams, 2007; Gamble, 2006). Observe the example below.

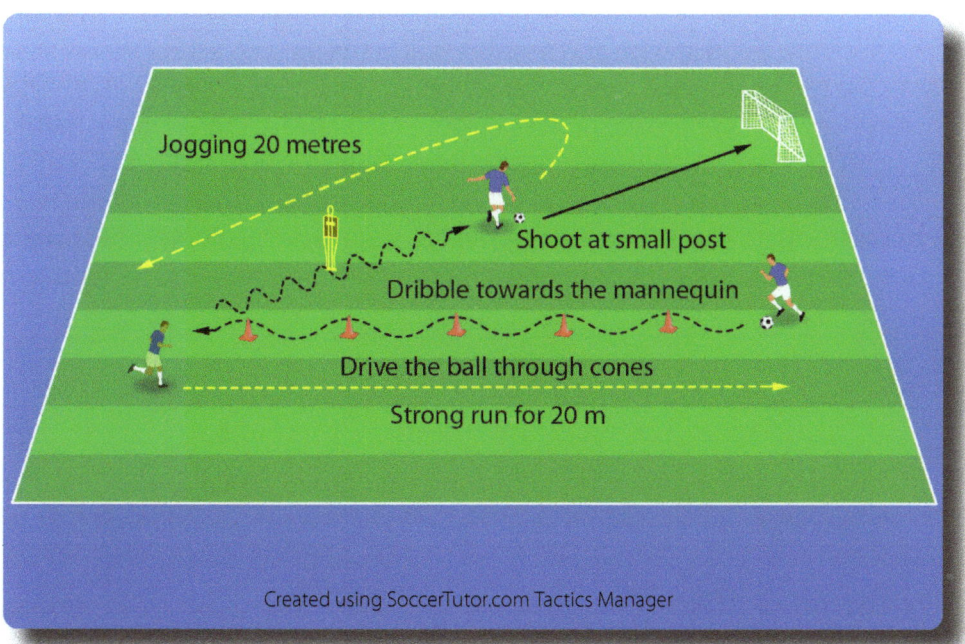

Image 24: *Endurance Exercise.*

These forms of training have a huge disadvantage because they train one (physical ability) or two aspects of performance (physical ability + technique) but they can not address all four pillars of performance. This results in a waste of precious time as well as creates training loads that you will need to address. If our objective is simply an overload in endurance capacity we can use this

Physical abilities

type of stimulation, but when we are trying to maximize performance and create team improvement, then we will need to introduce a different type of stimulation.

When the training process simulates the conditions of a game, then the foundations are set for the correct execution of the elements used in training.

If you train like the image above then you are only training aspects of physical abilities or physical and technical abilities. So what do you do when you want to train your players in the same way that they play?

The holistic training approach offers more benefits to the players since along with their endurance abilities, (which simulates the game and the needs of the game perfectly) it also trains their technical, tactical and mental elements. We describe training as being holistic when it simulates the conditions of the game and competitive action as much as possible. A player that must be positioned and receive and pass the ball in the right space in order to reach the goal of the exercise, creates the conditions for improving his overall performance as well as approaching his performance plateau. Therefore the method that should be predominantly used when training in specialized endurance is the use of small sided games where we place specific formations of the teams that participate at specific dimensions and within a defined timeline for execution, as well as using specific restrictions and setting specific goals for the exercise.

For the Endurance Block we can use three different numerical proportions of players:

(A) Small-sided games 11 vs. 11 to 8 vs. 8 players with approximately 100 m^2/player. For example in a 10 vs. 10 players small-sided game format (20 players x 100 m^2 = 2.000 m^2) the dimensions that must be set are approximately an area of 40 m x 50 m = 2.000 m^2.

In such games the internal load (with the use of a GPS system that also monitors heart rate) is usually low to medium ~70-90% MHR with average intensity close to 80% MHR (with the players working below 100% of their VO2max). The external load (as observed through advanced GPS systems) is also defined as low to medium with the total distance covered being less than or equal to 100m/min. Hence, in a 9 vs. 9 players small-sided game format with 2 sets of 8 mnutes each, the total distance each player will cover is equal to approximately 2 x 800 m. = 1.600 m.

Below you can see an example of training with a small-sided game format of 11 vs. 11 to 8 vs. 8 players.

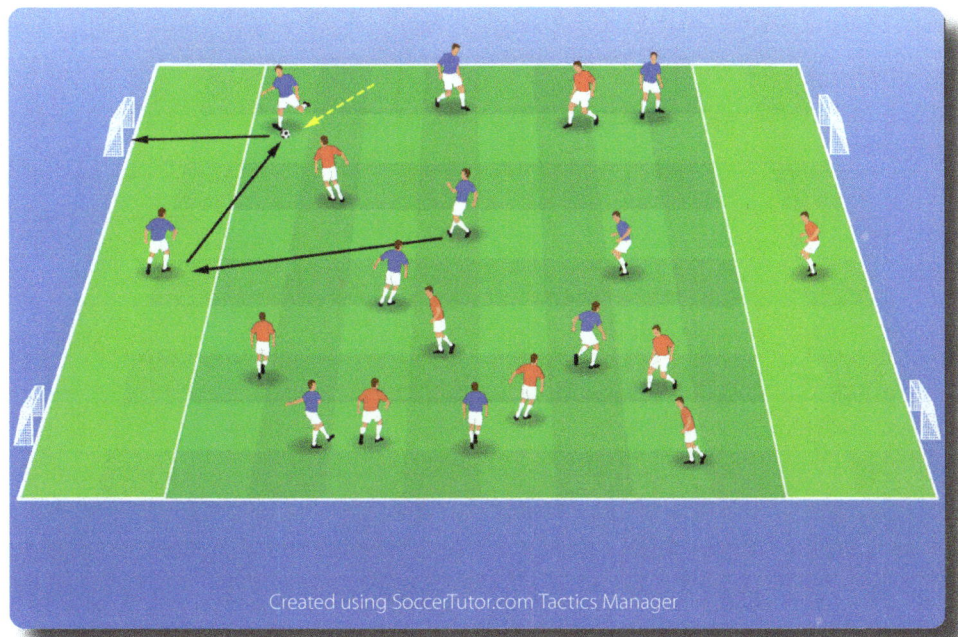

Image 25: *Exercise with small sided games.*

Large number of players lowers the executed amount of explosive actions during the drill, which results in a low level of accelerations-decelerations and direction changes. The duration of these small-sided game formats is higher (usually 6'-15- per set) and they impact mainly on the ability to maintain actions for a prolonged amount of time (meaning the player should be able to last 90' of action). An example of small-sided games with these ratios and their GPS and telemetric heart rate results is below.

Physical abilities

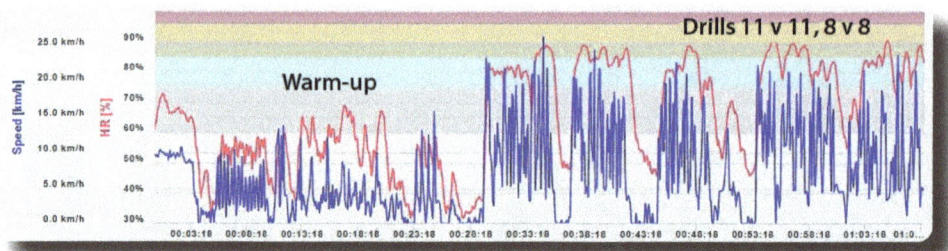

Image 26a: *GPS and HR results during small-sided game.*

(B) Small-sided games with 7 vs. 7 to 4 vs. 4 players with approximately 100 m²/player. For example in a 6 vs. 6 players small-sided game format (12 players x 100 m² = 1.200 m²) the dimensions that must be set are approximately an area of 40 m x 30 m = 1.200 m².

In such games the internal and external load is found to be medium to high. The heart rate is approximately 85-95% MHR and each player will approximately cover an average of 100m/minute. Hence, in a 6 vs. 6 players small-sided game format with 2 sets of 8 minutes each, the total distance that the players will cover is equal to approximately 2 x 400 m. = 800 m.

When speeds are higher so are the accelerations and decelerations which results in a higher load on muscles-tendons and joints will also increase both the external and internal training load.

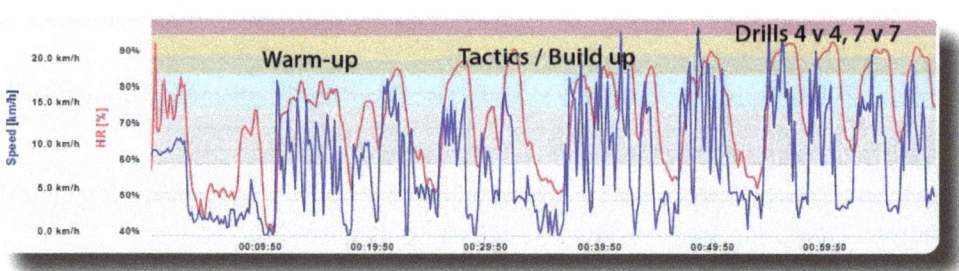

Image 26b: *GPS results during small-sided game.*

The duration of these small-sided game formats is medium (usually 3'-6' per set) and their impact is both on the ability to maintain activity for a prolonged period of time as well as on the ability to quickly recover from one action to another. An example is shown in the image below.

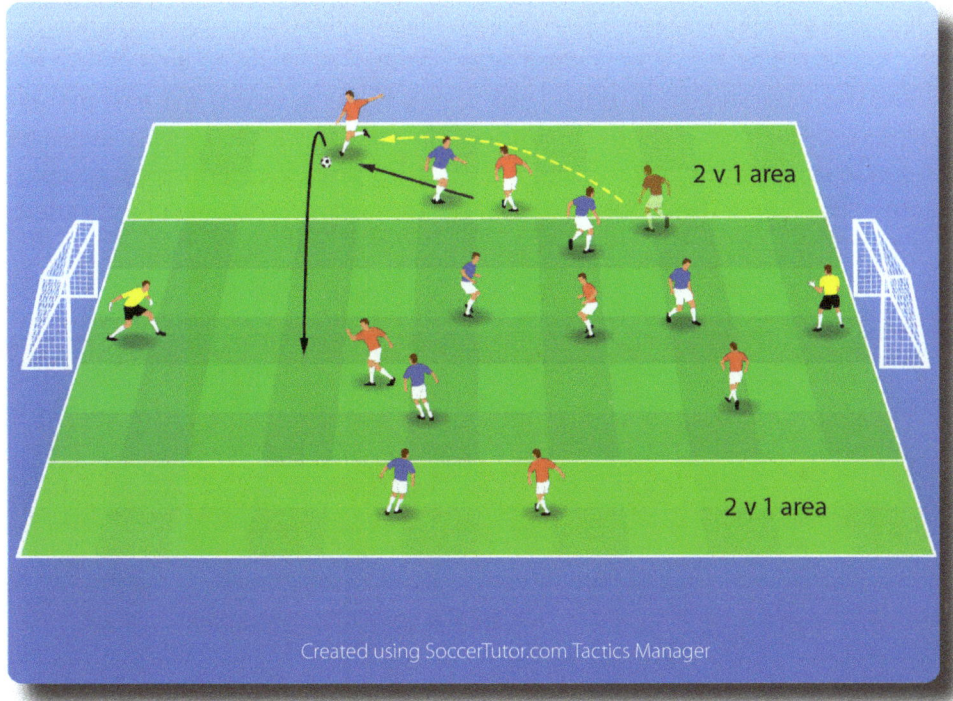

Image 27: *Exercise with small-sided game.*

These small-sided game formats are considered to be the most efficient when training endurance in combination with technical-tactical and mental elements of the game for the periodization model that is analyzed in this book.

The benefits of using small-sided game formats with higher number of players can be during 11 vs. 11 tactical training during the weekly training cycle as long as there are not too many interruptions by the coach during their execution, thus when using a 3+2 training week schedule 7 vs. 7 to 4 vs. 4 small-sided game formats are the best and most common without this meaning that other small-sided game formats cannot be used during the various weekly microcycles.

Physical abilities

(C) Small-sided games 3 vs. 3 to 1 vs. 1 players, are associated with high external loads and are considered dangerous for injuries when involving players without adequate fitness foundations. The benefits of these formats can be met (albeit not completely) by 4 vs. 4 to 7 vs. 7 small-sided game formats, thus their use should be limited to once every 15 or 30 days. We must mention that some physical fitness coaches avoid them completely.

During 3 vs. 3 to 1 vs. 1 small-sided game formats in an area of 100m^2 or less, the internal and external load is very high especially the external load since the levels of phosphocreatine and intramuscular pH are very low, whilst high levels of blood lactate, intramuscular lactate and adenosine monophosphate often limit the duration that the exercise can continue and thus internal load of the players may not be high.

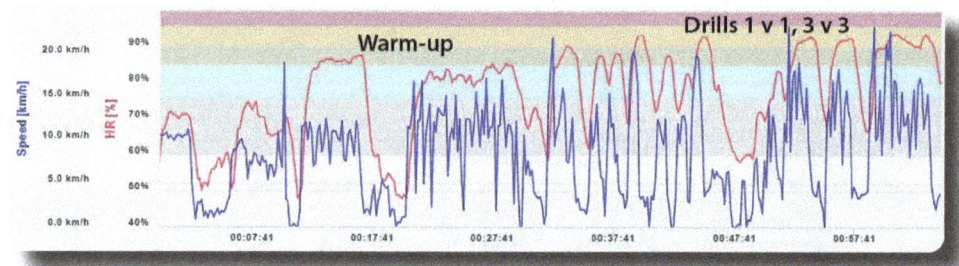

Image 28: *GPS results during small-sided game.*

In order for a player to partake in such rigorous training, we must be very cautious and also make sure that the player is well prepared, has not been recently injures or has a history of muscular injuries. He must also have a high level of tolerance to anaerobic training.

Note that when an athlete makes a change of direction when he is at maximum speed, the forces are up to 5 times his body weight (see images below).

physical abilities

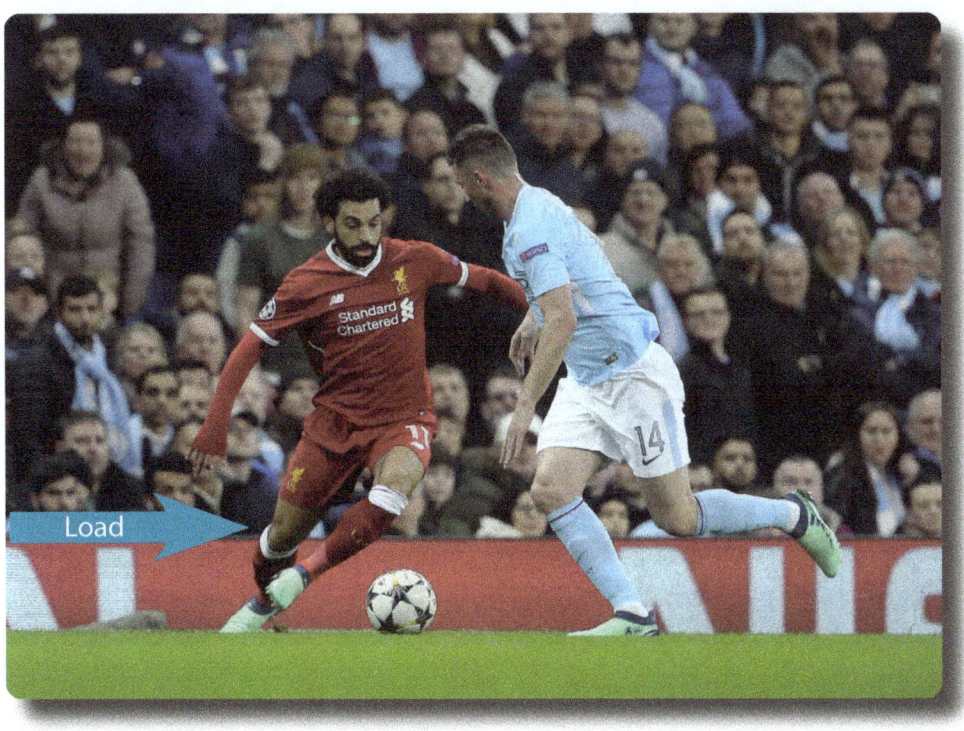

C PHYSICAL ABILITIES

Physical abilities

The reason we include this type of training in our exercise regiment is to be able to simulate the physical demands that the player will have to respond to during the actual game, to quickly recover between explosive actions and to train the body to handle large amounts of lactic acid. The duration of these small-sided game formats is short (1'-3') and their main goal, in relation to physical traits, is to increase the number or actions that the player can execute in a specific amount of time. Because these formats simulate situations that occur during a game (1 vs. 1, 2 vs. 1, 3 vs. 2, 3 vs. 3) and for which the player will be called upon to find solutions (see image below), they will also affect the player's technique and tactical decision-making.

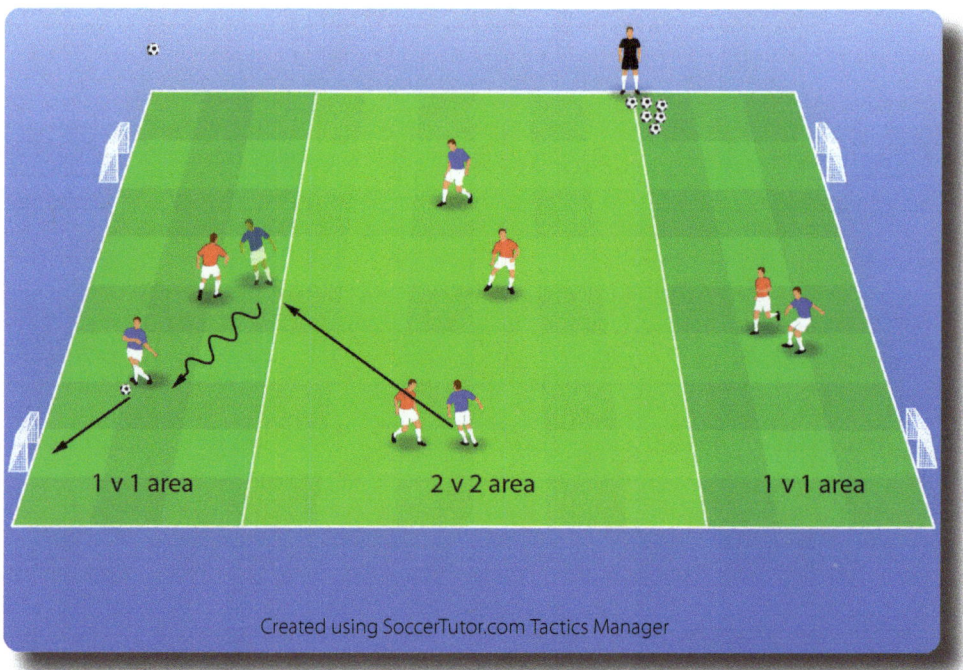

Image 29: *Drill with 1 vs. 1 to 3 vs. 3.*

The philosophy behind a 3 week periodisation training plan is multidimensional and is not only based on a vertical axis of the 3+2 week training but also on the horizontal axis of the regular season. The mathematical sequence which is applied is meant to prepare but also increase the stimuli with a "wave-like" form in order to constantly improve the players specific ability. This sequence must include periods of progressive increase in training loads but also periods of recovery in order to protect the player from reaching a performance plateau (a stagnation of performance).

What we are essentially doing is improving the player's physical fitness by disrupting the homeostasis of his body via increased training load, while making sure he always has adequate time for recovery.

"Wave-like" sequence of endurance training stimuli

During the 1st week of implementing our periodization model, the overload for endurance is applied to the players with at least 48 hours between the two stimuli. The first training unit be applied in the middle of the week with a higher volume closer to the day of the game but with reduced volume. The second training unit is specially designed (lower volume) and "strategically" placed within the weekly cycle, in order to avoid accumulating fatigue (from the previous training unit with the same stimulation) that may result in affecting the upcoming game in a negative way. Keeping a balance between inducing and managing fatigue during the weekly cycle is a basic component of a training model. It has been observed that when we overload the player's physical fitness training (2 training units per weekly cycle) and combine it with an intense game schedule, the players are at the risk of non-functional overreaching and in reality their physical fitness level will decrease over time (Kraemer et al., 2004).

So for example, if we have a game on a Sunday, followed by another game on the following Sunday, then Mondays and Tuesdays should be devoted to the recovery of the player to his initial physical state. On Wednesday we apply a specialised endurance training unit through 5 vs. 5 players small-sided game forma with 2 GK in a 40 x 30 m^2 area for 4 x 4' with 2' breaks in between. On Thursday our main focus is technical-tactical. On Friday we re-apply an endurance training unit with 6 vs. 6 players small-sided game format in a 30 x 40 m^2 area for 2 x 3' and a passive break of 2' in between sets. On Saturday we must actively rehabilitate and get ready for the game on Sunday.

Physical abilities

Below we present the fluactations of the 4 vs. 4 to 7 vs. small-sided games volume. These fluactations of the training volumes refer to the "wave-like" sequence we analysed and will be used accordingly throughout the season by the trainers of the team.

	1st Endurance Block	2nd Endurance block	3rd Endurance Block	4th Endurance Block
Wednesday (max)	20'	30'	25'	35'
Friday (max)	10'	10'	10'	10'
	Game simulation exercises	Game simulation exercises	Game simulation exercises	Game simulation exercises

Wednesday: 5 vs. 5 and 2 GK, 4x4' and 2' break
Friday: 6 vs. 6, 2x3' and 2' break

	5th Endurance Block	6th Endurance block	7th Endurance Block	8th Endurance Block
Wednesday (max)	20'	30'	25'	35'
Friday (max)	10'	10'	10'	10'
	Game simulation exercises	Game simulation exercises	Game simulation exercises	Game simulation exercises

The volumes of the small-sided games are presented in the table below, depending on various player formats, the intensity target and the break times.

Methodology of main endurance training methods in soccer with the use of small sided games					
Number of players	Intensity	Duration	Repetitions	Break	Total duration
11 v 11, 8 v 8	80-90% MHR	6'-15'	1-8	1'-2'	20'-60'
7 v 7, 4 v 4	85-95% MHR	3'-6'	4-8	1:½ to 1:1 per repetition	20'-40' incl. breaks
3 v 3, 1 v 1	Maximum effort	20''-3'	2-4 sets 4-8 rep/tions	1:1 to 1:3 per rep. 3'-5' per set	max 20' incl. Breaks

An example of a complete weekly cycle design with an endurance emphasis will be presented in the following chapters.

Strength

Strength is perhaps the most neglected area in soccer training even in teams at the highest level. Many physical conditioning coaches prescribe exercises for injury prevention or work on speed-power which is soccer strength and more likely to be needed during a game and the goal of which is for the player to apply the maximum amount of strength in the shortest amount of time in order to gain an advantage against his opponents.

In practice, when physical conditioning coaches do not emphasize strength equally to the other two physical abilities of endurance and speed, they basically depend on the innate characteristics of their players (whether they are naturally strong or powerfull) and less on their work with the players. There are also cases where teams with high level players have these skills at an extreme level and are therefore the team staff neglect training them for improvement. It is therefore dangerous to try to copy these training methods and philosophies since the players of your team may be substantially different to the players of the team you are trying to copy.

Physical abilities

The 3 week periodization plan of improvement takes under consideration the interference phenomenon and places the strength training depending on the training block that we are at. Therefore the training of various skills interfere, but work harmoniously in order to improve the performance of the player (Stewart, 2014).

The time between the two strength training units in the 2nd week of our periodization model must be at least 48 hours. If we assume that our games are every Sunday, then on Wednesday we will execute complex strength training and on Friday we will focus on reactive strength (see an example in chart below).

Complex strength training is defined as training where one strength exercise (with resistance of 75% of one maximum repetition) is followed by a biomechanically similar exercise.

The rationale in complex strength training, is that the strength exercise activates the Central Nervous System to a great extent so that more type IIb muscle fibres are activated, potentially increasing the performance levels of the subsequent plyometric exercise.

Reactive strength training is defined as plyometric training, in which force is created through the process of the stretch-shorten cycle.

The table below presents the allocation of these training block in the consecutive strength blocks. The training blocks refer to the "wave-like" mathematical sequence that develops over time and that will be used accordingly by the physical conditioning coaches throughout the season.

	1st Strength Block	2nd Strength Block	3rd Strength Block	4th Strength Block
Wednesday	Complex Strength Training	Complex Strength Training	Complex Strength Training	Complex Strength Training
Friday	Reactive Strentgh Training	Reactive Strentgh Training	Reactive Strentgh Training	Reactive Strentgh Training

Wednesday:
3 sets x 4-6 repetitions, squats with barbell +6 jumps with 2 feet over 50 cm obstacles.
3 sets x 4-6 repetitions, bench press + 6 push up claps
Friday:
3 sets x 6 repetitions, jumps with 2 feet over 20 cm-40 cm obstacles.

	5th Strength Block	6th Strength Block	7th Strength Block	8th Strength Block
Wednesday	Complex Strength Training	Complex Strength Training	Complex Strength Training	Complex Strength Training
Friday	Reactive Strentgh Training	Reactive Strentgh Training	Reactive Strentgh Training	Reactive Strentgh Training

During the complex strength training session, execute the basic squatting exercises with barbell and bench weights after your athletes have taken a 1 repetition max test. If for practical reasons you cannot take the max test, then work according to the maximum repetitions with the maximum weights that the players can handle in order to complete the necessary repetitions defined by the program with the best possible technique.

In the second block of our periodization plan we focus on complex strength training with loads higher than 75% of 1RM (1 repetition maximum) in order to maintain strength levels. This is then followed by reactive strength training (plyometrics). An example of complex strength training is presented below.

A. Barbell back-squat: *3 sets x 4-6 repetitions.*

Physical abilities

B. Box jumps: *3 sets x 6 repetitions.*

C. Bench press: *3 sets x 4-6 repetitions.*

D. Clap push-ups: *3 sets x 4-6 repetitions.*

During complex strength training you can add secondary strength exercises as well as core exercises. The exercises that will complement the 2 main sections are selected by the physical conditioning coach based on his personal opinion on what would be most useful. An example is provided below.

	Exercises	Sets and Repetitions	Break
Exercise 1	Barbell squat +Jumps over obstacles (lower body)	3 x 4-6 +6	2'
Exercise 2	Plank with foot motion (core)	3 x 30''	15'
Exercise 3	Bench press + clap push-ups	3 x 4-6 +6	2'
Exercise 4	Lunges on bosu ball (lower body)	3 x 12	1'
Exercise 5	Pull-up (upper body)	3 x 6-8	1'
Exercise 6	Rusian twists with medicine ball 5 kg (core)	3 x 30''	15''

Allow a 1 minute break between the strength exercise and the corresponding plyometric exercise (exercises 1 and 3). By stimulating the muscles in this way, we maintain the curve of maximum strength at a high level (Bompa & Buzzichelli, 2015) as well as train the particular skill with a low load and without disrupting the neuromuscular system to a high degree and hence leading our training process towards the goal of the soccer specific strength (Bompa & Buzzichelli, 2015).

We must make sure to keep a practical approach when strength training in order to avoid a common complaint made my players that may sometimes feel they lose their sense of "connection" with the ball. A good way to avoid this phenomenon, is to complement their strength training with a small and simple set of exercises with the ball (if the teams training center facilities allows of course) for example a rondo game or 5 vs. 2 (image 30) so that the Central Nervous System may once again adjust to the particular kinetic skills of the sport.

Even when training for peaking, the ability of strength may take years to reach its highest levels. The rationale of training in soccer is not to train each of the 4 skills separately, but instead to maximise the athletes total performance based on the four pillars as they have been previously analysed. Thus a

Physical abilities

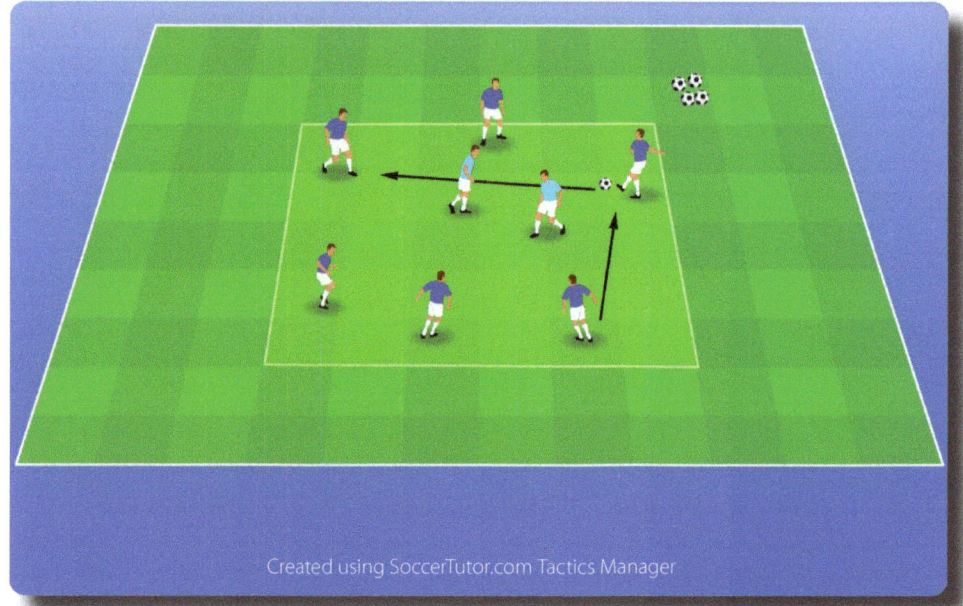

Image 30: *Rondo drill.*

periodized model that trains strength seperately from the other components of performance would not translate into the expression of the full strength potential.

Training for maximum strength can result in variations to the total performance and can raise the chances of injury. Many athletes have not been taught the correct execution of specific actions and others have limited training experience, therefore training stimuli with very heavy loads (>75% 1RM in exercises such as squats and deadlifts) there is a high probability that in a group of 22-28 athletes, most will either not be able to complete the exercise or will experience negative side effects (muscular pain, loss of neuromuscular coordination) which are so extensive that they make this type of training unnecessary (with the exception of periods with no competitive obligations or soccer training i.e. transition period).

Many sports scientists support that loads higher than 75% are required in order for an athlete to train sufficiently for maximum strength (Gamble, 2006; Peterson et al., 2004). Some support that 1 maximum strength training unit per month is enough to maintain strength levels. With our 3 week periodization model we ensure a safe sequence while constantly setting the foundations and requirements for maintaining and improving soccer specific strength strength. For example, when applying this training model to a Superleague team, countermovement jump (CMJ) improved during the competitive season (September to January) both for regular starters (41.9 ± 3.9cm vs 43.4 ±3.8cm) as well as for non-starters (41.6±4.8cm vs 44.3 ± 5.7cm) (Papadakis et al., 2011). The countermovement jump is considered to be a reliable way to measure lower body specific strength for professional players (Turner & Stewart, 2014), which based on our data, is not easy to improve within the competitive season. For example, both a high intensity training model (3 half squats at 4RM) every week or every two weeks for 12 weeks (Ronestad et al., 2011), as well as a training plan with a medium to very high training volume (20,8±11,9 to 52,5 ± 42,8 minutes) (Mallo, 2012), failed to improve the countermovement jump after a 16 week competitive period (Lopez-Segovia et al., 2010). In fact, when training for 25 weeks with a single training unit per microcycle, the countermovement jump decreased at the middle of the competitive period (Silva et al., 2011).

The second strength training unit in the Strength Block focuses on reactive strength and is executed in the form of plyometrics. Reactive strength training is executed after a good warm up and before the main section. The volume and intensity is maintained at a low level (few jumps and low obstacles) and therefore does not have a negative effect on the technical and tactical elements that will follow. Adding sprints to reactive strength training is not necessary so the exernal loads can be even lower (see example of reactive strength training). Training with the use of repetitive stretch-shorten cycles has benefits in explosive power (or otherwise called "the first golden step") as well as improves the proper function of the muscles as well as endurance (through the increase of running economy) and the decrease of muscular injuries (Asadi et al., 2016; Rumpf et al., 2016; Bedoya et al., 2015; Barnes & Kilding, 2015; Markovic, 2007).

An example of reactive strength training can be seen on the next page (Image 31).

Physical abilities

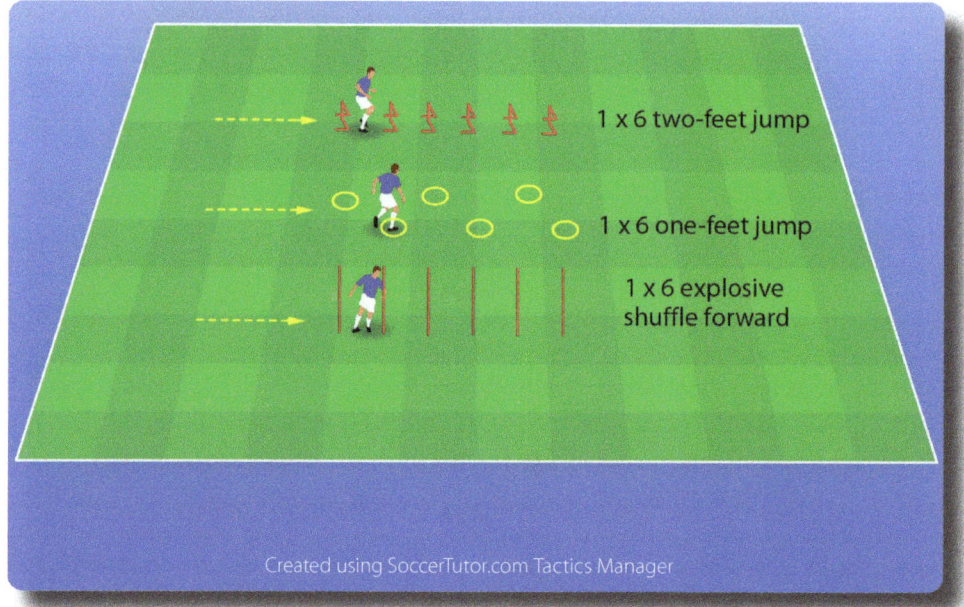

Image 31: *Reactive strength training.*

The main purpose of strength training is improving the soccer soccer strength, or otherwise speed-strength or power without excluding maximum strength, which is trained with loads higher that 75% of the 1RM during complex training.

During the competitive microcycle we do not need to include exercises for training muscle endurance during strength training because it is already covered during training. Running, directional changes, duels and other soccer actions, put the muscles under many low and medium loads during the course of one training unit.

We use this type of training during preparation season or whenever else we think it may be necessary (the return of an athlete after an injury, the addition of a new player etc.)

The sequence that we can use throughout the whole year by simply altering the % of RM, occurs after testing the players for 1 repetition maximum. Even if the test cannot be executed due to lack of time or practical difficulties, the players will observe improvement from one training session to another and they can try to execute exercises with a heavier load if you feel like they want the challenge and the exercise feels too "easy" for them. If this occurs, it means that there have been positive effects on the athletes body from the strength training, and that their maximum repetition has already increased.

Variations of load and volume during strength training, as well as the number of sets per exercise, are decided by the physical conditioning coach, as well as the decision to de-load their players due to bad weather conditions on the field or fatigue accumulating by repetitive game loads. In some exercises you might choose to have 1-3 repetitions depending on the total load of the athletes from training and playing. Many scientists support that even 1 set of squats may provide adequate stimulation for the maintenance of the specific skill over time.

Gradual alternation to the sequence of the load is intended to improve performance, hence the main target is to increase the soccer specific strength.

In the case that a double training is scheduled within the day (Soccer Training- Strength Training), it is wiser to execute strength training in the afternoon and soccer training in the morning. The mTORC1 enzyme, which is responsible for regulating protein synthesis in the human body, requires an adequate amount of protein which can be acquired through the consumption of a main meal (lunch). In addition, as long as soccer training is executed first and strength training is placed on a separate training unit following at least 6 hours of rest, the AMPK enzyme (enzyme responsible for regulating the adaptations of aerobic endurance) is activated immediately after the morning training and returns to regular levels as soon as the session stops (more or less 6 hours).

This way when the second training unit begins, the low levels of the AMPK enzyme will not interfere with strength training, since it has been observed that high levels of the enzyme block the increase of the levels of mTORC1 which would limit the strength training adaptations (Stewart, 2014). Another advantage is that the evening strength training will not reverse the benefits of their morning training that could be caused by fatigue and a "fatigued" neuromuscular system. Papadakis et al., followed the above training sequence on professional players for approx. 20 weeks during the competitive priod, and observed an increase in both aerobic endurance (velocity at 4mM of lactate) and the ssoccer specific strength (countermovement jump) independent from the amount of time that each athlete participated in games.

As we mentioned earlier, you can always add a cycle of exercises, before or after strength training, that are designed to prevent injuries and serves as a

Physical abilities

warm up. Research has shown that the addition of these exercises to our routine for 5'-15' before our daily training (with the exception of the day of a game or the day of rehabilitation), can work synergistically in the aspect of strength and can be useful in the prevention of injuries. An example of training for injury prevention can be observed below.

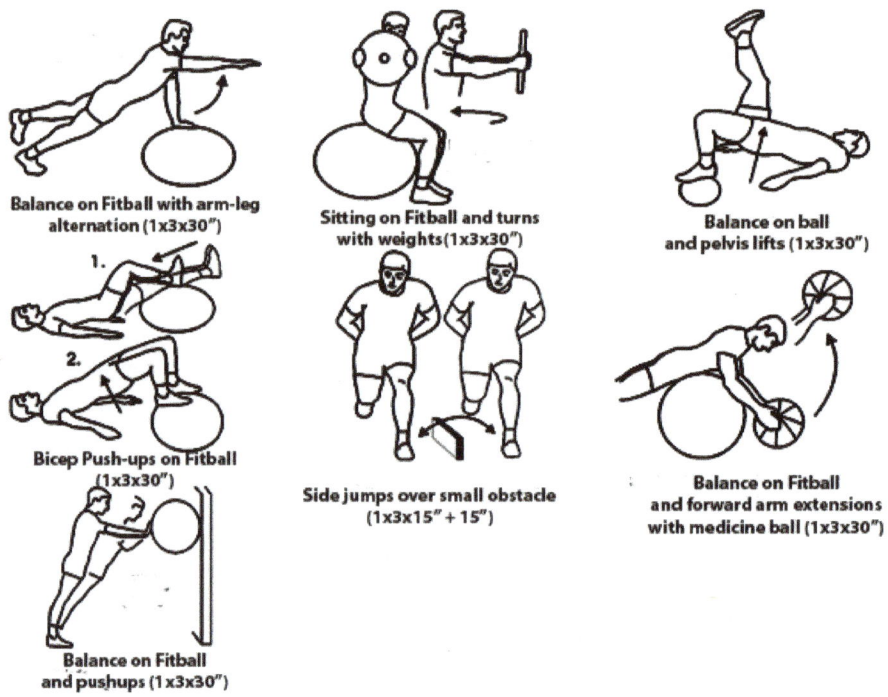

Image 32: *Exercises for injury prevention.*

Speed

This is the skill that gets paid with the highest price in modern soccer and that every coach looks for within his team. All the derivatives of speed (cyclic or acyclic speed, starting speed, speed of actions, maximum speed, mental speed, speed of thought etc.) are at the highest point of the players pyramid. No matter what form of soccer training we follow in the field, the skill of speed is sometimes trained more and sometimes less frequently.

Imagine how many times the players will be called upon to execute actions under the pressure of time during a 7 vs. 7 competitive game. For example their sprints, their decision making, the swift execution of a pass or drive. During 8 vs. 8 to 11 vs. 11 game formats, explosive actions are performed in large spaces which gives the players the opportunity to develop maximum- or just below maximum- running speed for quite a few meters (Morgans et.al., 2014). The allocation of training units that focus on speed derivatives must be done

Physical abilities

carefully and with close monitoring because it is very easy to cross the "red lines" of this particular training. It depends to a great degree, on the type of soccer training the player has during his weekly micro-cycle and whether we want to maintain or increase his abilities.

Importantly the training history of a player should not be overlooked, especially regarding strength, since greater strength training history is associated with greater tolerance in speed training as well as more potential for improvement (Gamble, 2011).

In our periodization model of improvement, the weekly microcycle will include two training units for speed. At mid-week we train our players for acceleration with sprints of 10-20 m. 1-2 sets x 6-8 repetitions with a 30"-1' break between the repetitions and a 3'- 5' break between sets. We must adapt our training for speed to the needs of the game as much as possible so we can combine it with agility and coordination skills. An example is presented elow.

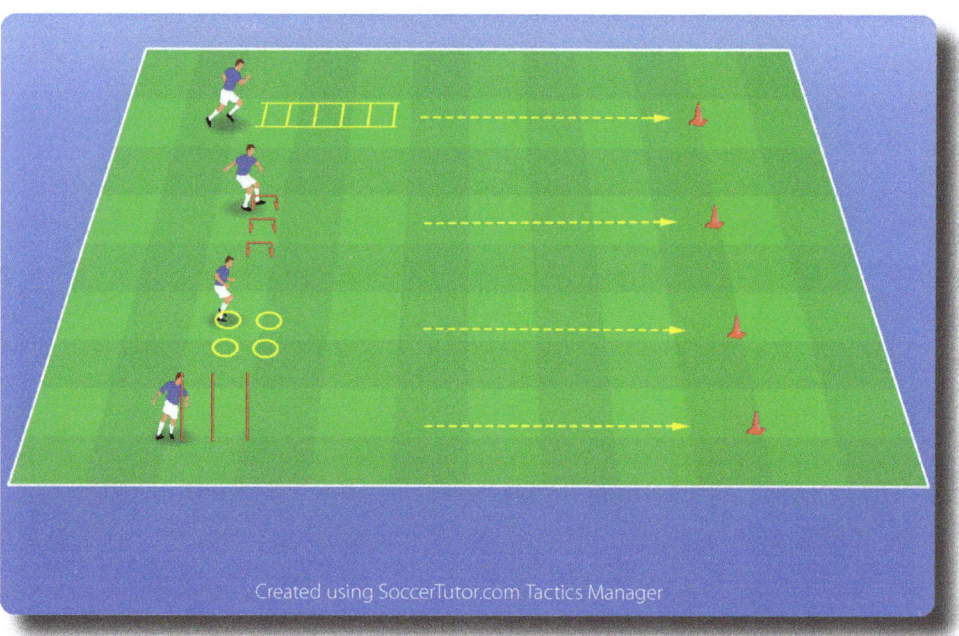

Image 33: *Speed training.*

The second training unit is the same one as in the previous blocks and it focuses on reaction speed. Forty-eight hours must seperate reaction speed from the preceeding speed training unit and is usually applied one (or two) days before the game. The main objective is to activate the Central Nervous System and to ensure the readiness of the players. A typical reaction speed scheme is 1-2 sets x 4-6 repetitions with a maximum distance coverage of 5m and a training example is provided in the image below.

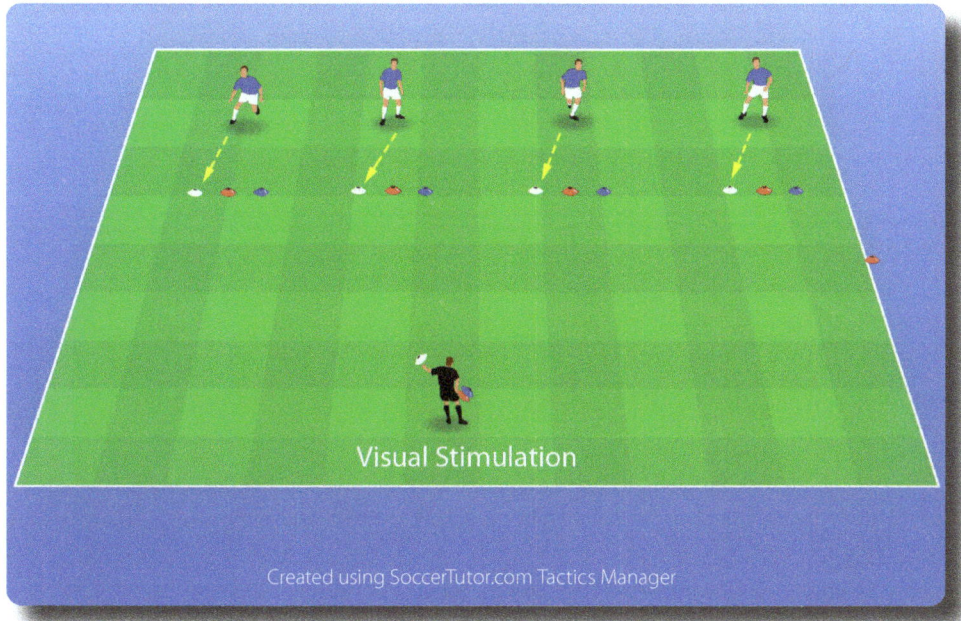

Image 34: *Speed training with visual stimulus.*

Many include reaction speed training within their regimen for speed training and often players are required to respond to an acoustic stimulation (whistling) from a standing position and execute a short sprint. Even though the athlete will execute a sprint of a maximum of 5 meters from a standing position, it is more of an exercise for training speed-strength with reaction (see image 35 with the speed-strength training spectrum) since the objective is to overcome the inertia that is caused by the weight of the body by applying force and speed to cover the specific distance. In this way, the starting speed of the athlete is trained as well as his reactive speed. When using this approach, and provided there is adequate distance to cover, it is good to remem-

PHYSICAL ABILITIES

Physical abilities

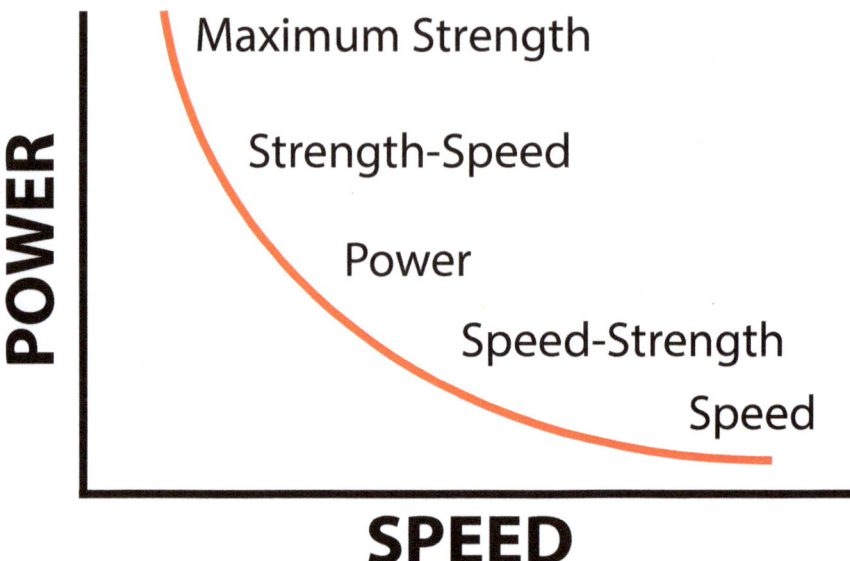

Image 35: *Training spectrum of strength and speed.*

ber alternating the leg that applies force to the ground per repetition in order to make sure that the load is shared and that there will be improvement.

When the objective of training is reaction speed, a fast reaction to an audio or visual signal is enough and they are not necessarily required to combine that reaction with the coverage of a distance. The skill of reaction speed can even be trained by pushing a button. During a game, the athlete is usually called upon to react to visual signals with specific kinetic models.

An example of reaction speed training without actually covering any distance can be seen below. The red player follows the steps of the blue player through cones with different colors for a specific amount of time (4-6 repetitions x5")

Image 36: *Reaction speed drill.*

The neuromuscular system must be alert and a good way to keep it alert is to provide a training stimulation of reaction speed the day before the official game. During the reaction speed training it is not always necessary to provide a stimulus by covering distance since the goal is the fast transfer of the information from the neurons in the brain to the muscles and not actually moving for a specified distance (Gamble, 2011).

Generally speaking, training for speed does not affect your players in terms of the internal load, but the neuromuscular fatigue that may follow could affect their overall performance. This is why the third microcycle of training and particularly that of training for speed, is considered to be the most difficult both in regards to the attention that must be paid when applying it, as well as in regard to the consequences of that training. In some cases, asking for that extra sprint may not be just as negative for your athletes as it is to under stimulate them and hence leaving them unprepared for what will follow.

The limits to which we need to work especially in the field of speed, can be set with the use of up-to-date technology in GPS monitoring systems which assist us in carefully observing the results of our training. We must always keep in mind the potential adverse effects of over-training and the negative affect

Physical abilities

on the overall performance of the player as well as individually on each of the 4 pillars of performance. Of course we need to stimulate and prepare the athletes' body for the needs of the game, but we must also take into account the stimulation that we are applying at each moment and the training load that the athlete receives during his soccer training (these are questions that we physical conditioning coaches are called upon to answer each day).

Additional training above the acceptable levels with explosive actions may induce neuromuscular fatigue thus having a negative impact on our performance graph. In addition, accumulation of intense concentric and eccentric contractions, raises the possibility of muscle injuries.

In practice, training is not a theoretical model in which we follow numbers and compartmentalise the separate characteristics of our players. Instead, it is a constant mixing of all 4 pillars of performance (technique-tactics - physical abilities - mental and psychological abilities) with the goal to reach the maximum possible expectations based on our players genetic material, while at the same time providing individualized training for each one of our athletes.

Synopsis

The image below provides a conceptual synopsis regarding the 3 week physical abilities periodization model (plus 2 optional weeks of maintenance and recovery). A thorough analysis of the model was provided in previous chapters emphasizing the sequence of the training interventions; especially the alternating nature of the overloading component that prevents excessive training loads.

Every type of training stimulation needs a particular period of time in which it's levels must be maintained. For example, in order to stabilize the ability of Maximum Strength, we need to subject our players to this type of stimulation at least once a month. The image above shows us how following our periodization model we can ensure that. The reason that I focus on Maximum Strength is precisely because of its important place in the total performance of the player compared to the other two strength qualities (muscular endurance and speed-power) - (Haff & Nimphius, 2012; Turner, 2009; Cormie et al., 2011). It is the only ability that we can improve simultaneously to the other two, if we

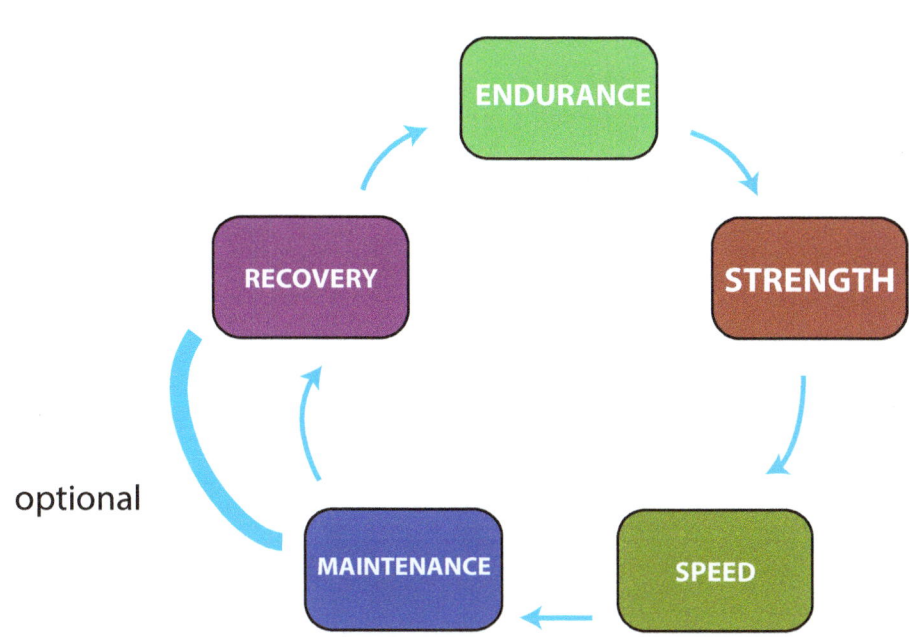

Image 37: *Blocks in the periodization model.*

place it at the base of our pyramid and treat it as essential. In fact in some cases, the increase in Maximum Strength alone, can result in a concurrent increase of speed-strength or athletic performance (Cornie et al., 2010a; Cornie et al., 2016b; Stone et al., 2002).

For example, when training athletes with low levels of strength, the implementation of maximum strength training was more effective that ballistic strength training while executing vertical jumps with or without external resistance (Cormie et al., 2010a). Within the soccer practice though, stimulation is not applied with loads that are targeted in the development if maximum strength but with submaximum loads that simultaneously improve the speed-strength characteristics of the kinetic skills (Bompa & Buzzichelli, 2015).

Essentially, speed is never neglected due to the nature of modern soccer training, but it is overloaded on the third week in an attempt to make adjustments and improvements.

Whilst endurance is overloaded during the first week of the periodization model (Endurance Block), endurance training (general to specific) continues throughout the 3-5 week mesocycle as well as throughout the competitive

Physical abilities

period. Within every training unit there are elements that stimulate endurance adaptations to various degrees.

The application of the training stimulus should always be done in consideration of the various training loads that the athlete has accumulated as well as the various types of training that he performs in order to choose the most appropriate training at the right moment and maximise the total soccer performance. Do you want a player that improved one characteristic or someone who became a better soccer player overall?

planning

Planning

Federations announce their annual regular season schedule, either at the beginning of the season or during the season and once the dates are announced you should start planning your teams preparation. The choice of using the periodization training method presented, serves as a coaching system for in-season improvement by helping trainers bring their soccer players to the desired level. Every three (3) weeks we can execute the specific regimen and by closely monitoring, we will be able to maintain the results. Following the three blocks (Endurance Block, Strength Block, Speed Block) we can either continue with a Maintenance Block (classic microcycle see image 38) or with a Recovery Block where the team has to execute only tactical and technical drills without any specific focus or overloading of physical attributes. This block serves as a general recovery for the athletes body and we even avoid strength training since it has specific stages and requires consistent rest times. In addition tak-

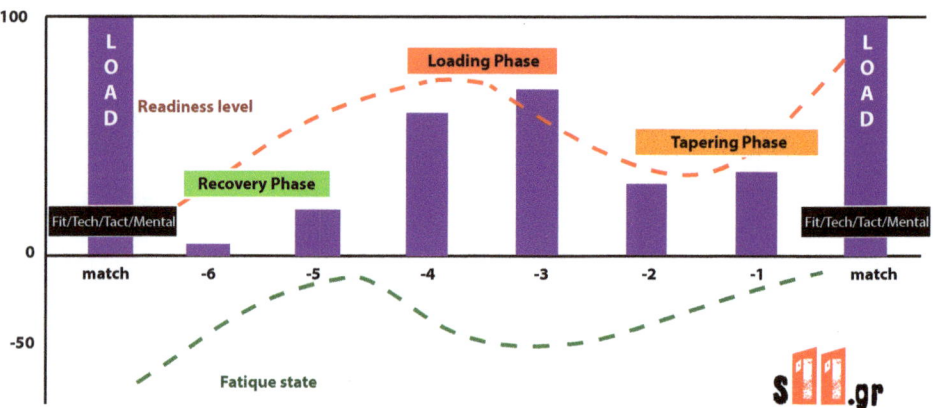

Image 38: *Training microcycle.*

ing into consideration the external load imposed onto the players during small sided games with low player ratio, actions such as directional changes with submaximal or maximal velocity are associated with large force generation that may account 5 times a player's body weight.

During the Recovery Block, we focus on tactical training in order to not overload the players any further. They will maintain their levels through the specific tactics their coach will choose. Our concern is that long intermissions during the flow of specific tactical training should be avoided. Within Recovery Block, speed training is limited to reaction speed training before an official game in order to activate the neuromuscular system as long as it is done at a low intensity volume (e.g. 1 set x 4-6 repetitions).

Observing your players closely for signs of exhaustion can lead to making adjustments in order to satisfy the needs of your players at any given moment. This is a fact that we can not ignore when evaluating or designing our weekly training cycles.

The design of a periodization model is not intended to conform to a training sequence at any cost, but to function as a "living organism" ready to adjust to new circumstances that occur within a team during its regular season.

Create your own periodization plan for improvement and maximise your teams performance by realising your ideas and accomplishing your goals over time. The following pages present an example of a yearly plan designed around the official games for the Championship and Cup.

Planning

REGULAR SEASON								
MONTH	SEPTEMBER				OCTOBER			
WEEK	1st	2nd	3rd	4th	1st	2nd	3rd	4th
CHAMPIONSHIP GAME	Kick off	2nd	3rd	4th		5th	6th	7th
CUP GAME			Game					
TRAINING BLOCK								

REGULAR SEASON									
MONTH	NOVEMBER					DECEMBER			
WEEK	1st	2nd	3rd	4th	5th	1st	2nd	3rd	4th
CHAMPIONSHIP GAME	8th		9th	10th	11th	12th	13th	14th	
CUP GAME								Game	
TRAINING BLOCK									

REGULAR SEASON								
MONTH	JANUARY				FEBRUARY			
WEEK	1st	2nd	3rd	4th	1st	2nd	3rd	4th
CHAMPIONSHIP GAME	15th	16th	17th	18th	19th	20th	21st	22nd
CUP GAME		Game						Game
TRAINING BLOCK								

planning

REGULAR SEASON									
MONTH	MARCH					APRIL			
WEEK	1st	2nd	3rd	4th	5th	1st	2nd	3rd	4th
CHAMPIONSHIP GAME	23rd	24th	25th		26th	27th		28th	29th
CUP GAME									
TRAINING BLOCK	🟢	🟠	🟡	🔵	🟡(gold)	🔵	🟡(gold)	🔵	

REGULAR SEASON				
MONTH	MAY			
WEEK	1st	2nd	3rd	4th
CHAMPIONSHIP GAME	30th			
CUP GAME				
TRAINING BLOCK	🔵	🟡(gold)	🟡(gold)	🟡(gold)

Endurance Block — green
Strength Block — orange
Speed Block — yellow
Maintenance Block — blue
Restoration Block — gold

D PLANNING

Example of a complete weekly micro cycle for the Endurance Block

Day 1 • Sunday

Morning: Rest
Afternoon: Game

Day 2 • Monday

Day Off

Note: Day 2 and Day 3 can be reversed. Meaning that Monday can be the Day Off and Tuesday training in two groups or Tuesday can be the Day Off and Monday training in two groups.

Planning

Day 3 • Tuesday

Morning: Group A (those who participated in the game for > 45 minutes
- 1 x 10' general warm up (see image 39).

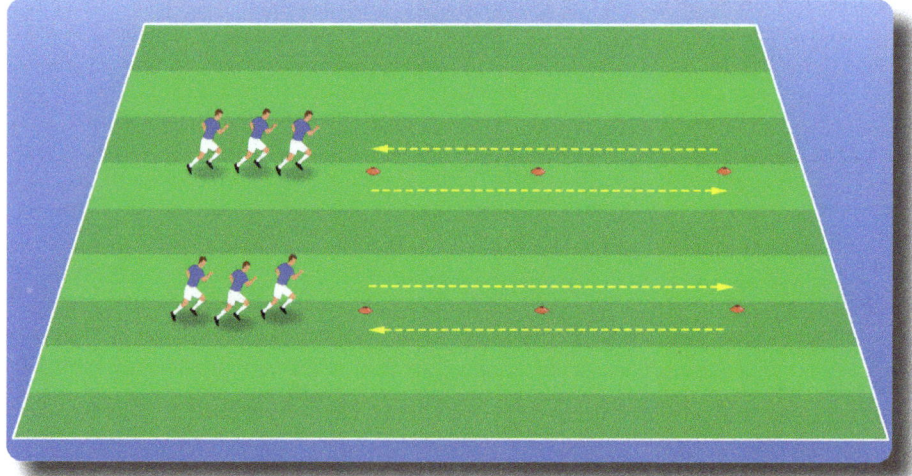

Image 39: *General warm-up drills.*

- 1 x 10' flexibility and agility exercises.
- 1 x 10' aerobic exercises with ball (technique) - (see image 40).

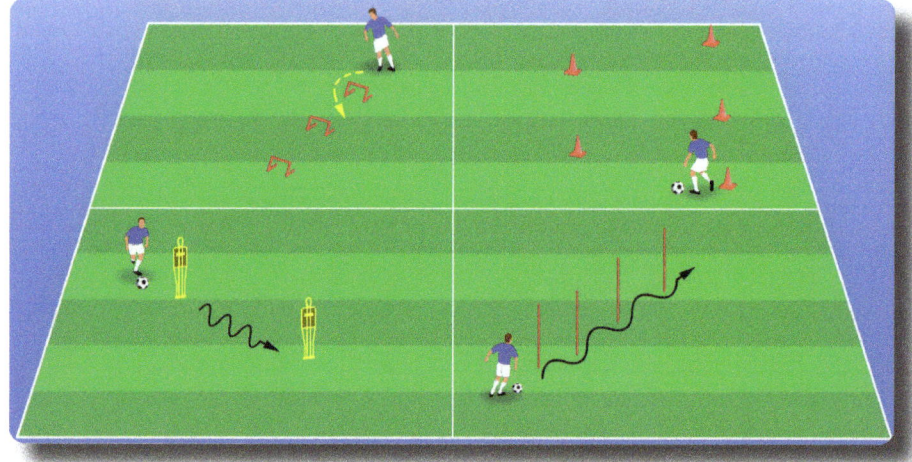

Image 40: *Low intensity aerobic drills with ball (technique) for the group that participated in game.*

Day 3 • Tuesday

- 1 x 10' aerobic exercise (running at 75% MHR) - (see image 41).

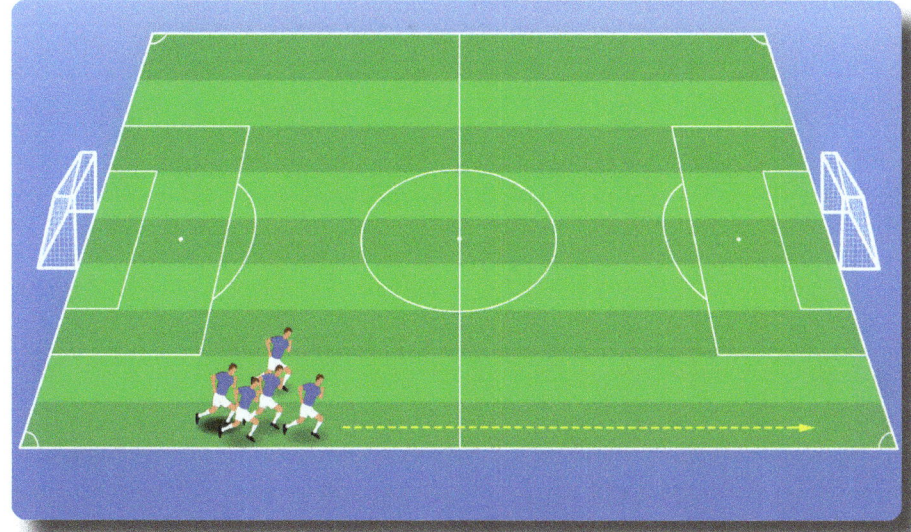

Image 41: *Low intensity aerobic running.*

- 1 x 10' recovery strategies.

Group B (those who did not participate in the game on Sunday or participated for < 45 minutes) follows the program below:

- 1 x 10' general warm-up.
- 1 x15' specific warm-up
- 4 x 4' with 2' stop. A simulation game with 4 vs 4 up to 7 vs 7 players and 2 goalkeepers.
- Additional endurance/strength/speed training depending on the level and the needs of the non-starter players.
- 1 x 5' low intensity running and cool off activity.

Afternoon: Rest

Planning

Day 4 • Wednesday

Morning:

- 1 x 10' general warm-up (see image 42).

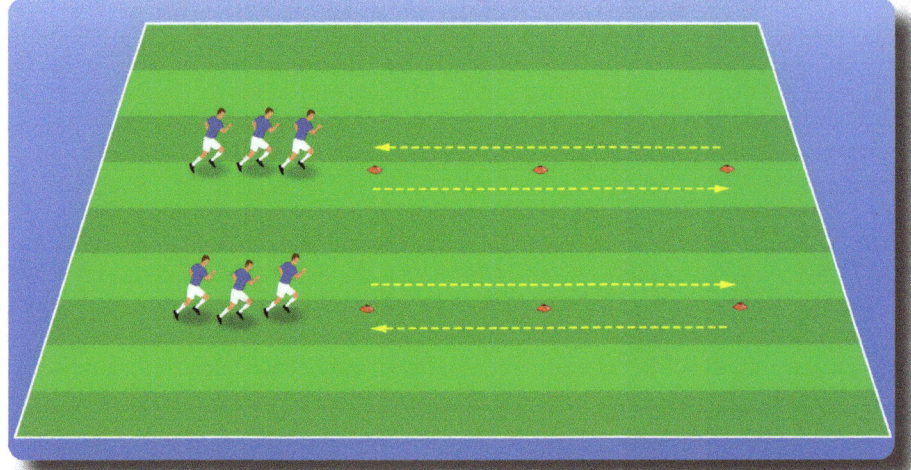

Image 42: *General warm-up drills.*

- 1 x 15' specific warm-up (see image 43).

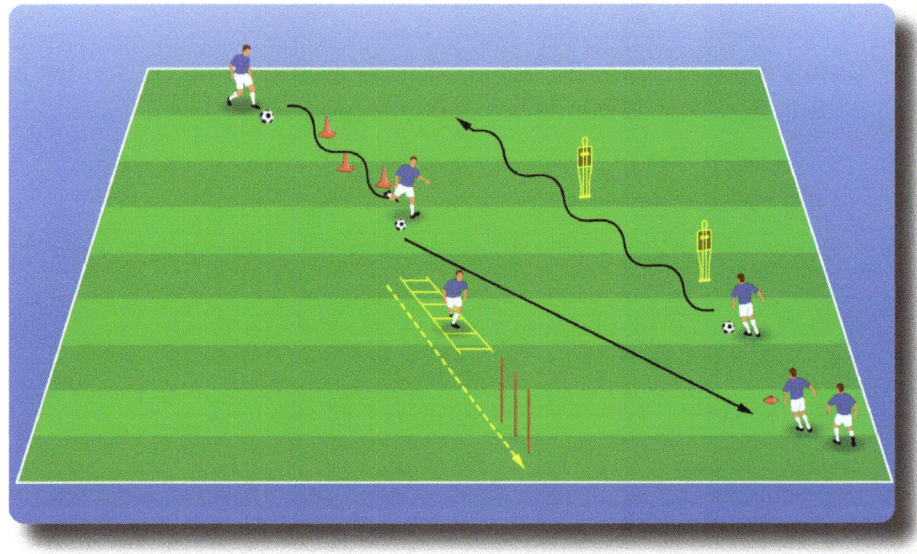

Image 43: *Specific warm-up drills.*

Day 4 • Wednesday

- 4 x 4' with 2' stop game simulation exercise with 2 goalkeepers (see image 44).

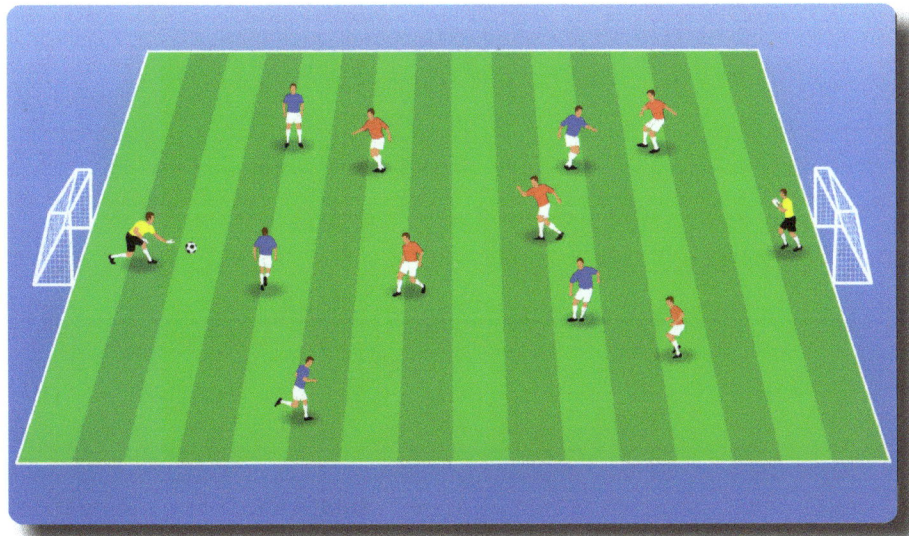

Image 44: *Small-sided game, 5 v 5 with 2 goalkeepers.*

- 1 x 5' low intensity running and cool off activity.

Afternoon:
- 1 x 10' general warm-up.
  1 x 30' strength training (see strength section for references to this specific training unit).
- 1 x 5' recovery strategies.

Planning

Day 5 • Thursday

Morning:

- 1 x 10' general warm-up (see image 45).

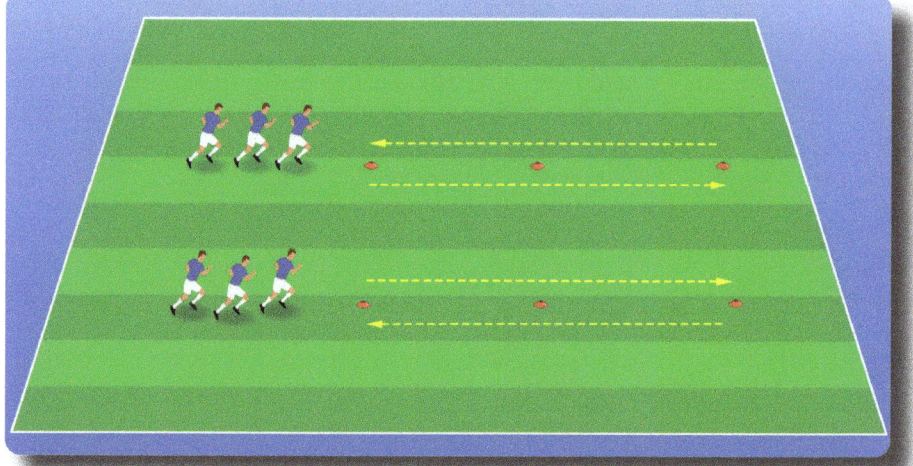

Image 45: *General warm-up drills.*

- 1 x 10' specific warm-up with game simulation exercises 9 vs 3 (see image 46).

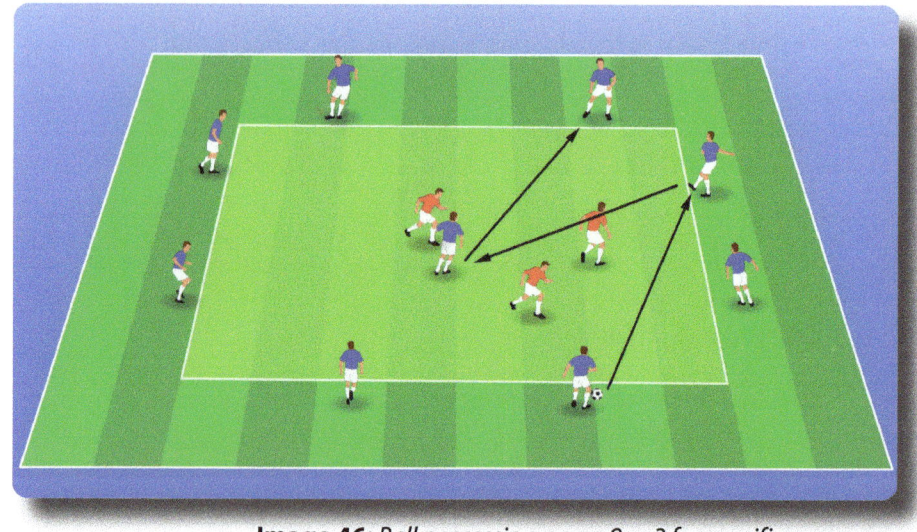

Image 46: *Ball possession game 9 vs 3 for specific warm-up.*

Day 5 • Thursday

- 2 x 10′ specific tactical training 11 vs 11 in the entire pitch with defensive and offensive game scenarios analysis (see image 47).

Image 47: *Specific tactics.*

- 2-3 x 10′ with 2′ break, free game 11 vs 11 at ⅔ or ¾ pitch (see image 48).

Image 48: *Free game 11 vs 11 at ⅔ pitch.*

- 1 x 5′ recovery strategies.   **Afternoon:** Rest

Planning

Day 6 • Friday

Morning:

- 1 x 15´ general warm-up (see image 49).

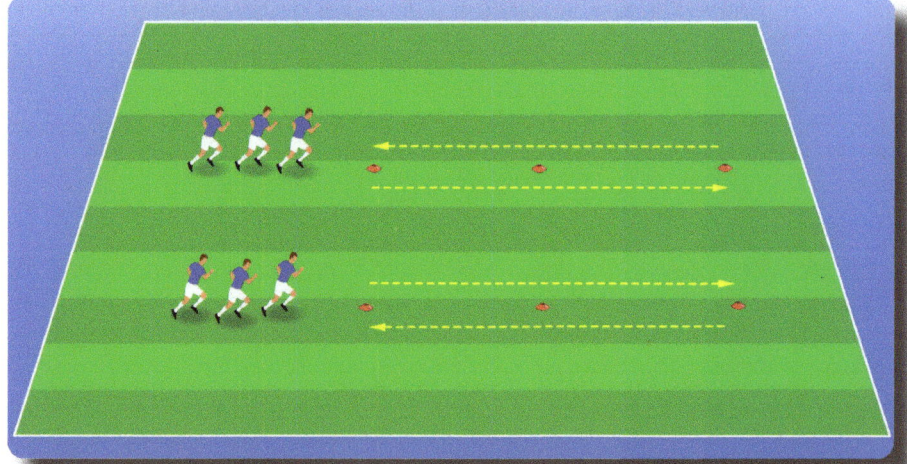

Image 49: *General warm-up drills.*

- 1 x 10´ technical training (varying), passing drills (see image 50).

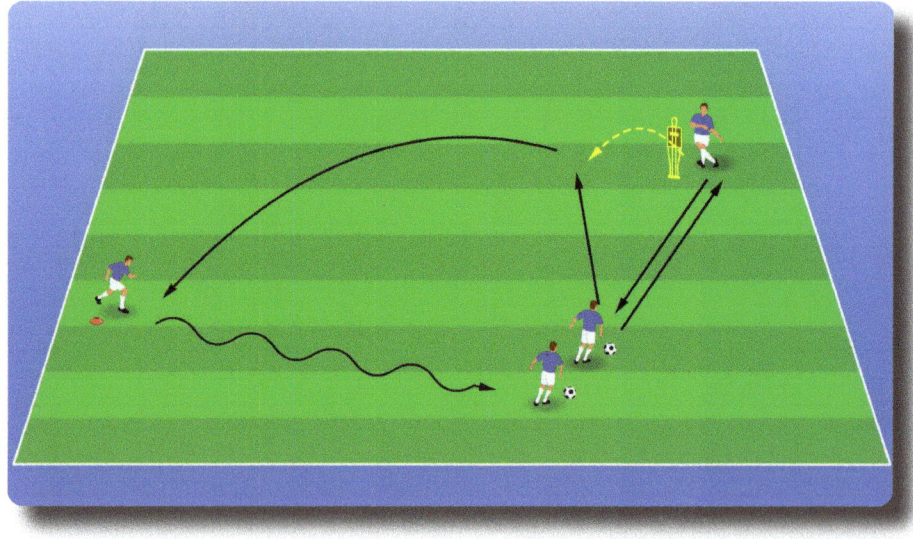

Image 50: *Passing drill.*

Day 6 • Friday

- 1 x 15' Technical/tactical drills with finishing (see image 51).

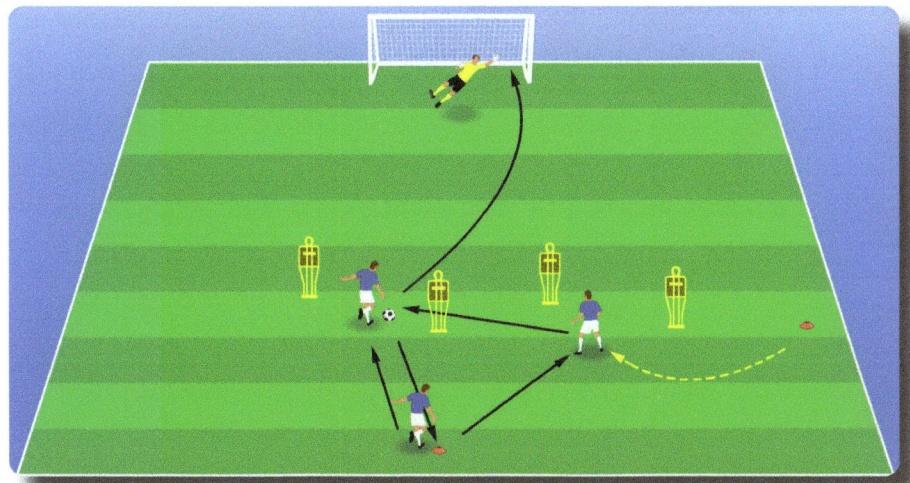

Image 51: *Technical and tactical drills with finishing.*

- 2 x 4' with 2' break, ball possession exercise 5 vs 5 with 10 supporters (see image 52).

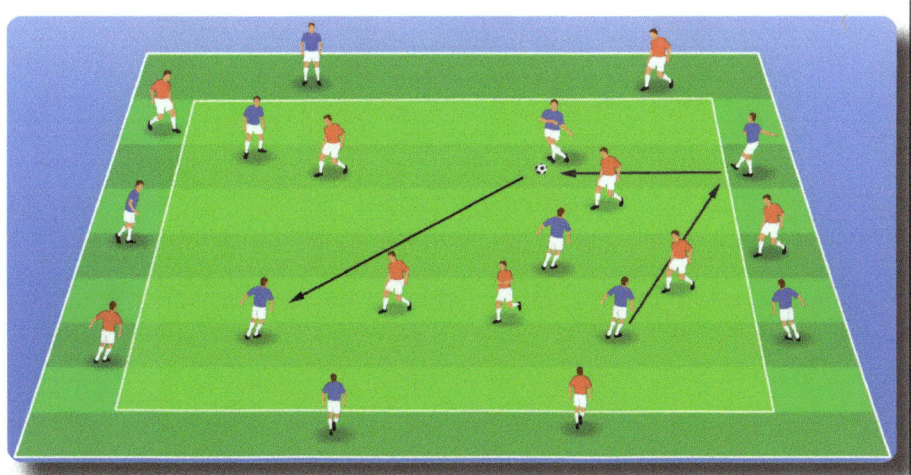

Image 52: *Game simulation exercise 5+5 vs 5+5.*

- 1 x 5' recovery strategies.

Afternoon: Rest

Planning

Day 7 • Saturday

Morning:

- 1 x 15' general warm-up (see image 53).

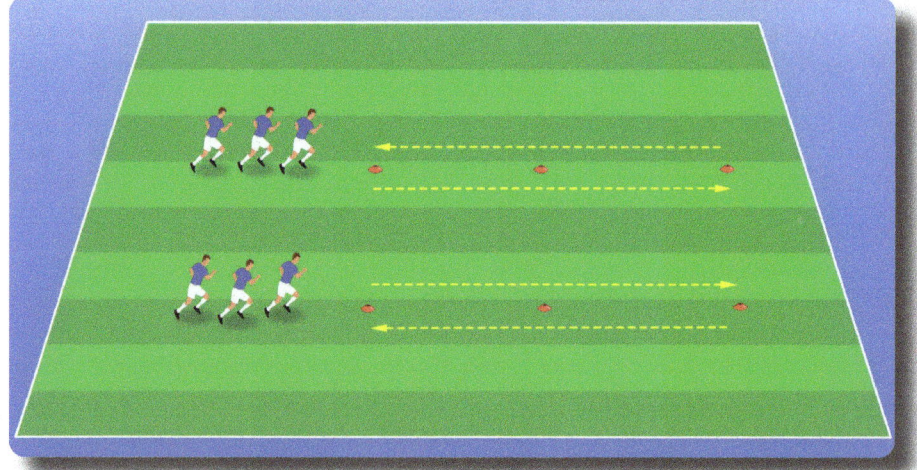

Image 53: *General warm-up drills.*

- 1 x 10' specific warm-up (see image 54).

Image 54: *Rondo 5 vs 2.*

Day 7 • Saturday

- 2 sets x 4 repetitions reaction speed training (see image 55).

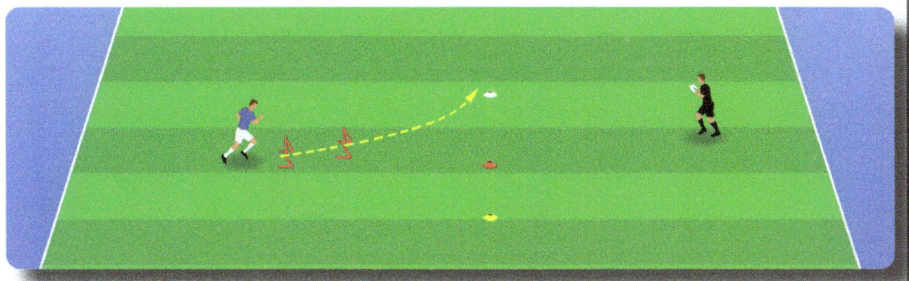

Image 55: *Acceleration and reaction speed training drills.*

- 4 x 2' with 1' break, 11 v 11 game with set pieces (defence -offence) in ½ pitch (see image 56).

Image 56: *Game plus set pieces drill.*

Afternoon: Rest

Example of a complete weekly micro cycle for the Strength Block

Day 1 • Sunday

Morning: Rest
Afternoon: Game

Day 2 • Monday

Day Off

Note: Day 2 and Day 3 can be reversed. Meaning that Monday can be the Day Off and Tuesday training in two groups or Tuesday can be the Day Off and Monday training in two groups.

Planning

Day 3 • Tuesday

Morning: Group A (those who participated in the game for > 45 minutes).

- 1 x 10' general warm up (see image 57).

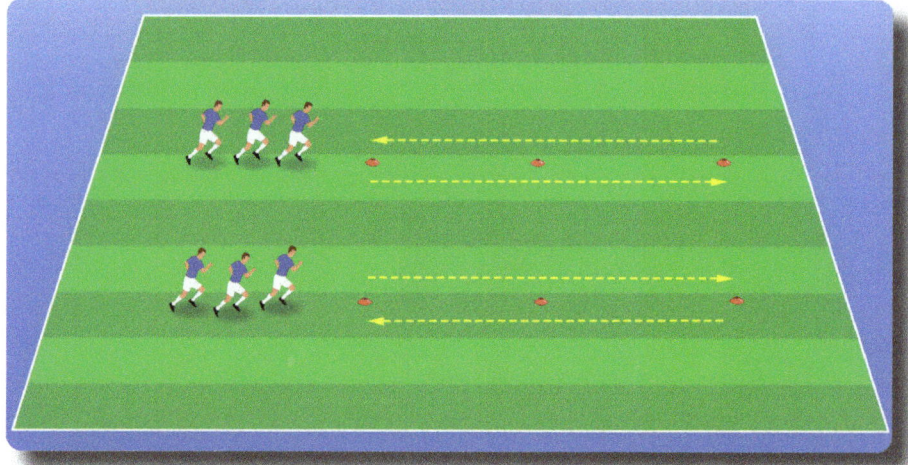

Image 57: *General warm-up drills.*

- 1 x 10' flexibility and agility exercises.
- 1 x 10' aerobic exercises with ball (technique) - (see image 58).

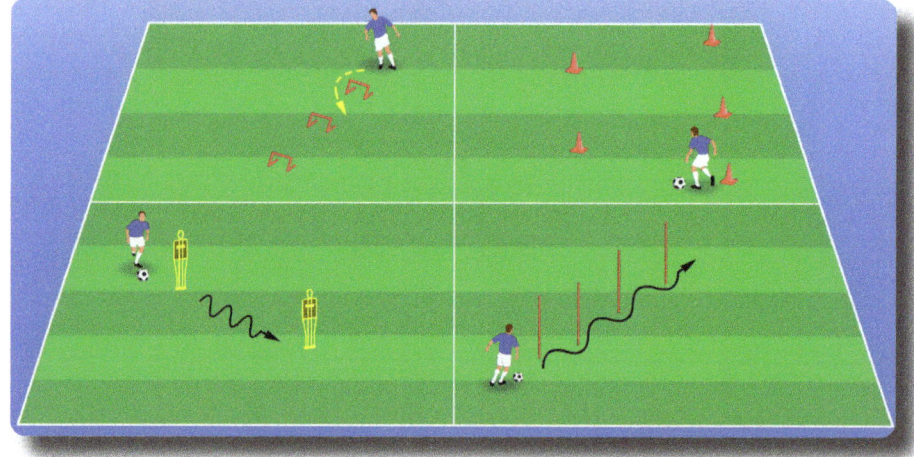

Image 58: *Low intensity aerobic drills with ball (technique) for the group that participated in game.*

Day 3 • Tuesday

- 1 x 10' aerobic exercise (running at 75% MHR) - (see image 59).

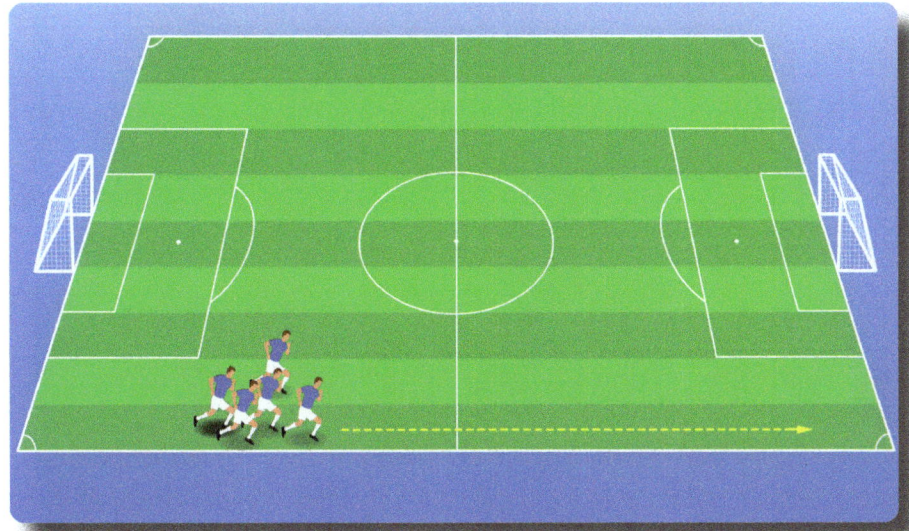

Image 59: *Low intensity aerobic running.*

- 1 x 10' recovery strategies.

Group B (those who did not participate in the game on Sunday or participated for < 45 minutes on Sunday) follows the program below:

- 1 x 10' general warm-up.
- 1 x 15' specific warm-up.
- 4 x 4' with 2' stop. A simulation game with 4 vs 4 to 7 vs 7 players and 2 goalkeepers.
- Additional endurance/strength/speed training depending on the level and the needs of the non-starter players.
- 1 x 5' low intensity running and cool off activity.

Afternoon: Rest

Planning

Day 4 • Wednesday

Morning:

- 1 x 10' general warm-up (see image 60).

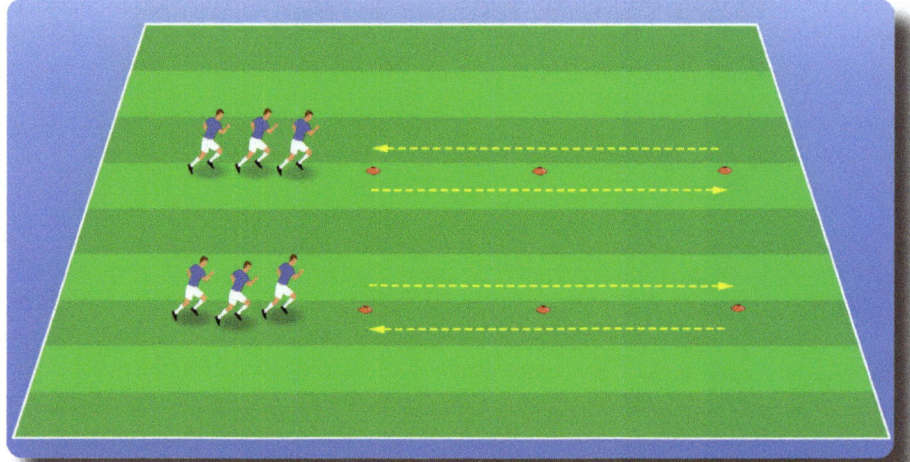

Image 60: *General warm-up drills.*

- 1 x 15' specific warm-up (see image 61).

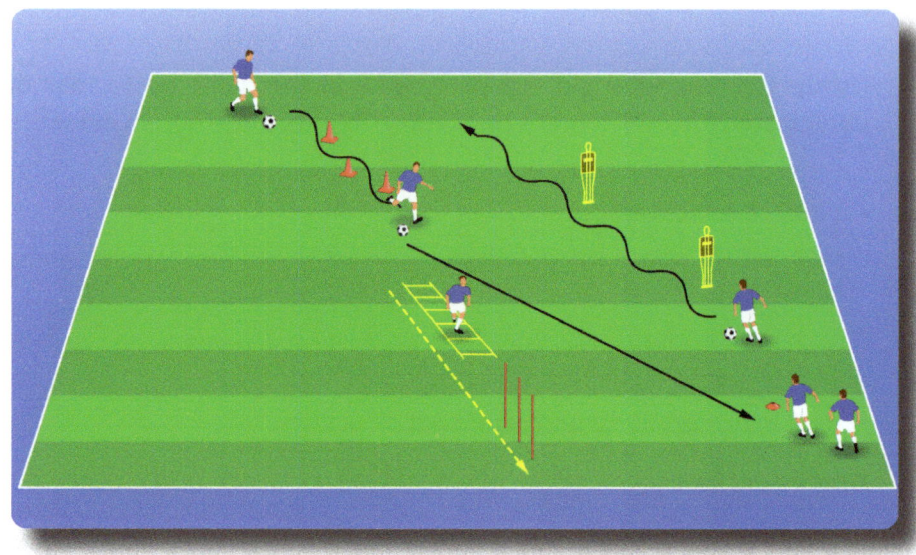

Image 61: *Specific warm-up drills.*

Day 4 • Wednesday

- 4 x 4' with 2' stop game simulation exercise with 2 goalkeepers (see image 62).

Image 62: *Small-sided game, 5 vs 5 with 2 goalkeepers.*

- 1 x 5' low intensity running and cool off activity.

Afternoon:

- 1 x 10' general warm-up.
- 1 x 30' strength training (see strength section for references to this specific training unit).
- 1 x 5' recovery strategies.

Planning

Day 5 • Thursday

Morning:

- 1 x 10' general warm-up (see image 63).

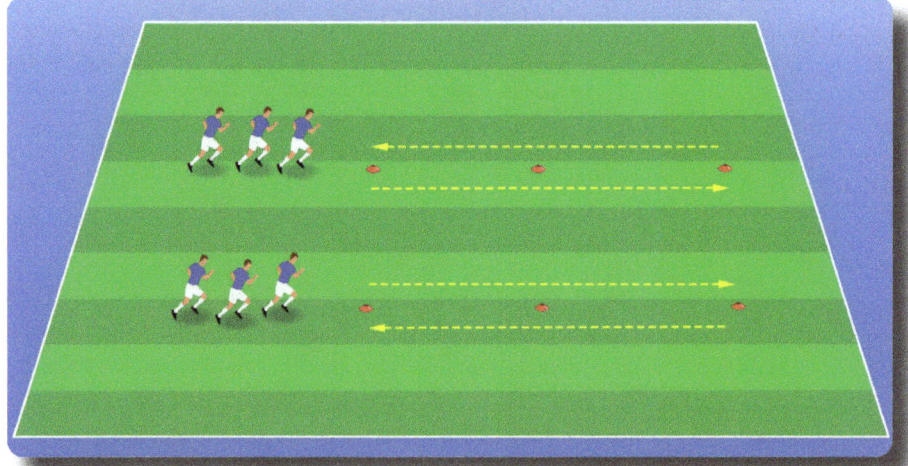

Image 63: *General warm-up drills.*

- 1 x 10' specific warm-up with game simulation exercises 9 vs 3 (see image 64).

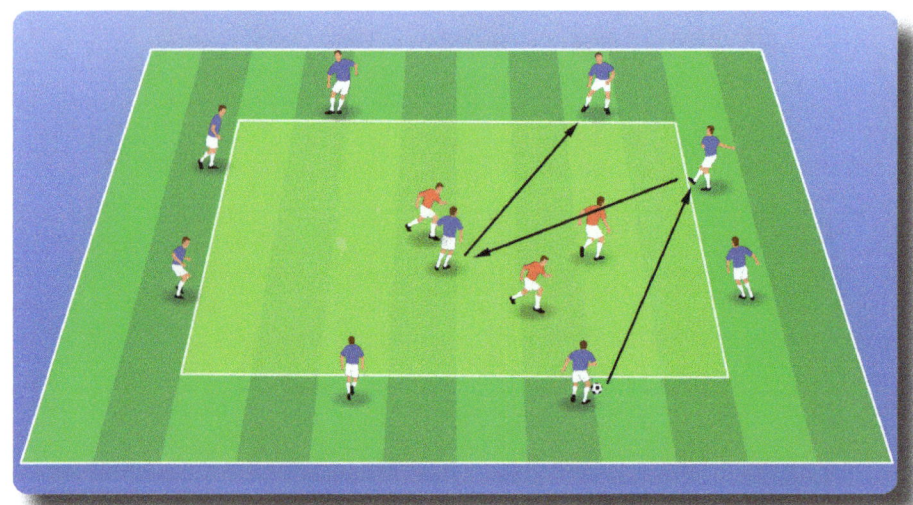

Image 64: *Ball possession game 9 vs 3 for specific warm-up.*

Day 5 • Thursday

- 2 x 10' specific tactical training 11 vs 11 in the entire pitch with defensive and offensive game scenarios analysis (see image 65).

Image 65: *Specific tactics.*

- 2-3 x 10' with 2' break, free game 11 vs 11 at ⅔ or ¾ pitch (image 66).

Image 66: *Free game 11 vs 11 at ⅔ pitch.*

- 1 x 5' recovery strategies.

Afternoon: Rest

Planning

Day 6 • Friday

Morning:

- 1 x 15′ general warm-up (see image 67).

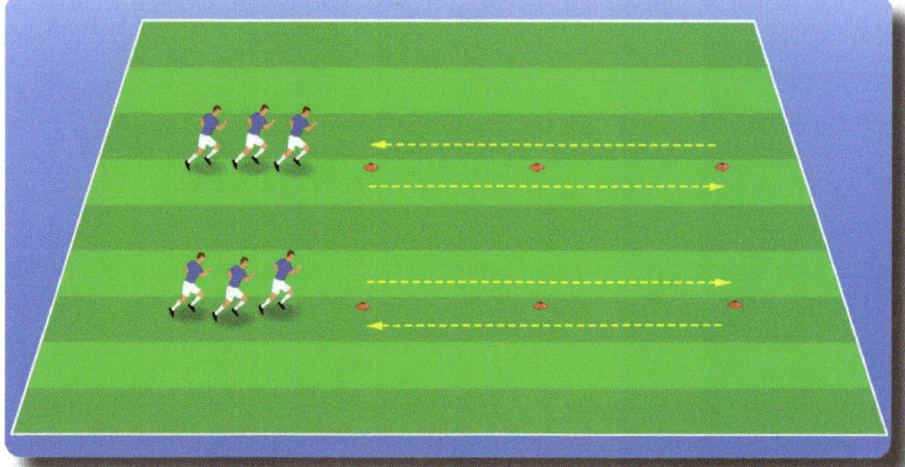

Image 67: *General warm-up drills.*

- 1 set x 3 repetitions reactive strength drills/exercises (see image 68).

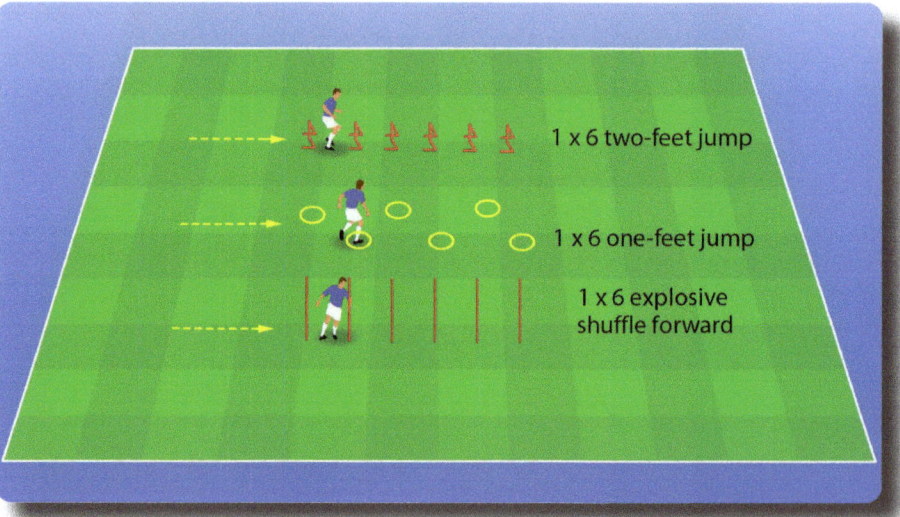

Image 68: *Reactive strength training drills.*

Day 6 • Friday

- 1 x 10′ technical training (varying), passing drills (see image 69).

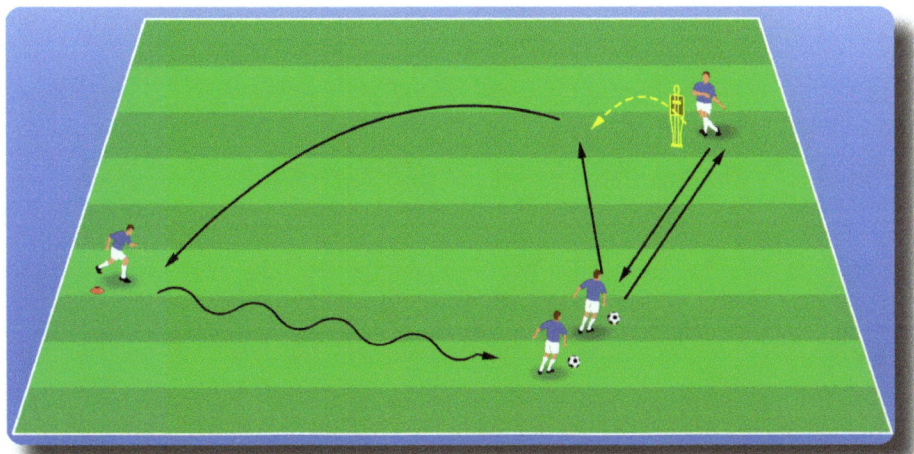

Image 69: *Passing drill.*

- 1 x 10′ finishing drills (see image 70).

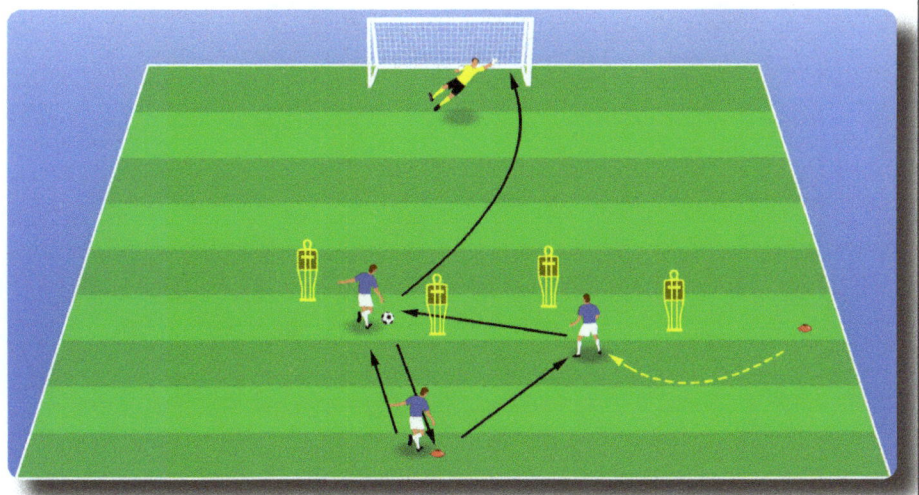

Image 70: *Technical/tactical drill with finishing.*

- 1 x 5′ recovery strategies.   **Afternoon:** Rest

Planning

Day 7 • Saturday

Morning:

- 1 x 10' general warm-up (see image 71).

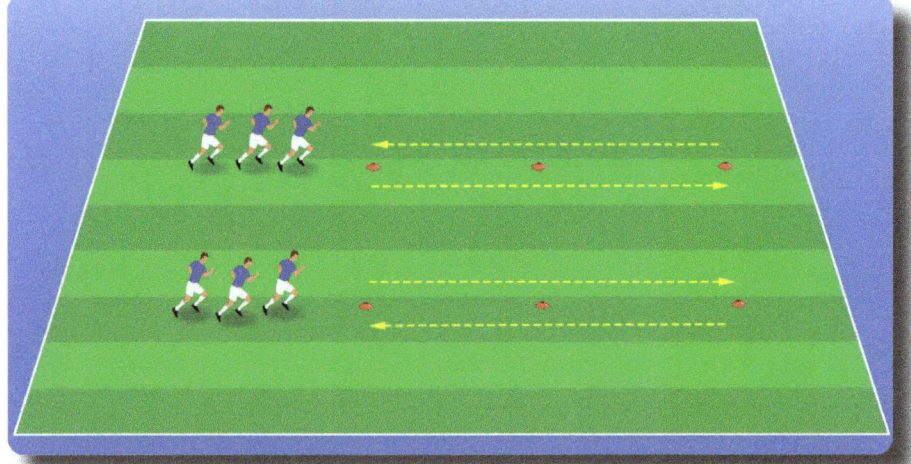

Image 71: *General warm-up drills.*

- 1 x 10' specific warm-up (see image 72).

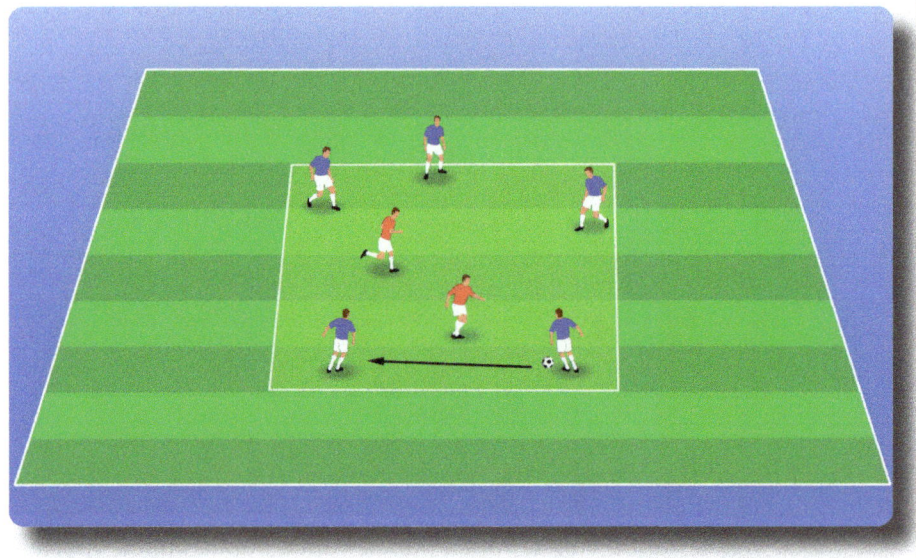

Image 72: *Rondo 5 vs 2.*

Day 7 • Saturday

- 2 sets x 4 repetitions reaction speed training (see image 73).

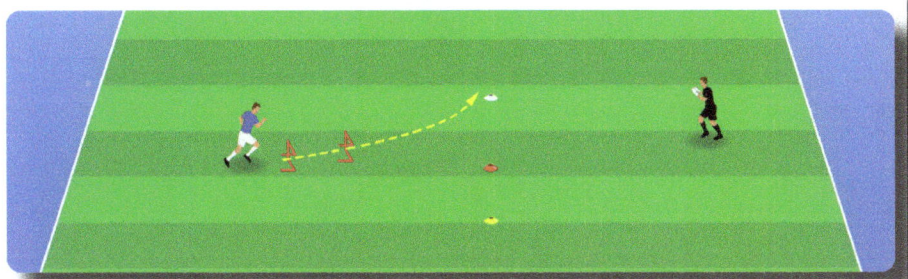

Image 73: *Accelerattion and reaction speed training drill.*

- 4 x 2' with 1' break, 11 vs 11 game with offensive and defensive set pieces in ½ pitch (see image 74).

Image 74: *Game plus set pieces drill.*

Afternoon: Rest

Example of a complete weekly micro cycle for the Speed Block

Day 1 • Sunday

Morning: Rest
Afternoon: Game

Day 2 • Monday

Day Off

Note: Day 2 and Day 3 can be reversed. Meaning that Monday can be the Day Off and Tuesday training in two groups or Tuesday can be the Day Off and Monday training in two groups.

Planning

Day 3 • Tuesday

Morning: Group A (those who participated in the game for > 45 minutes)

- 1 x 10´ general warm up (see image 75).

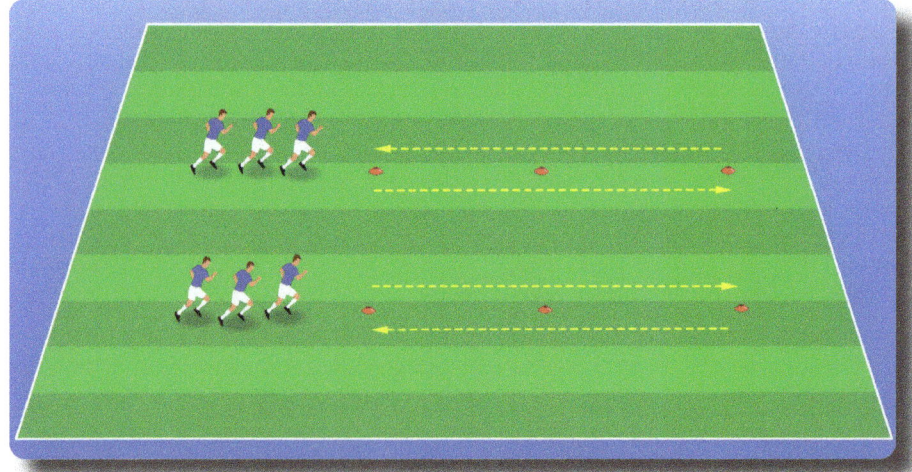

Image 75: *General warm-up drills.*

- 1 x 10´ flexibility and agility exercises.
- 1 x 10´ aerobic exercises with ball (technique) - (see image 76).

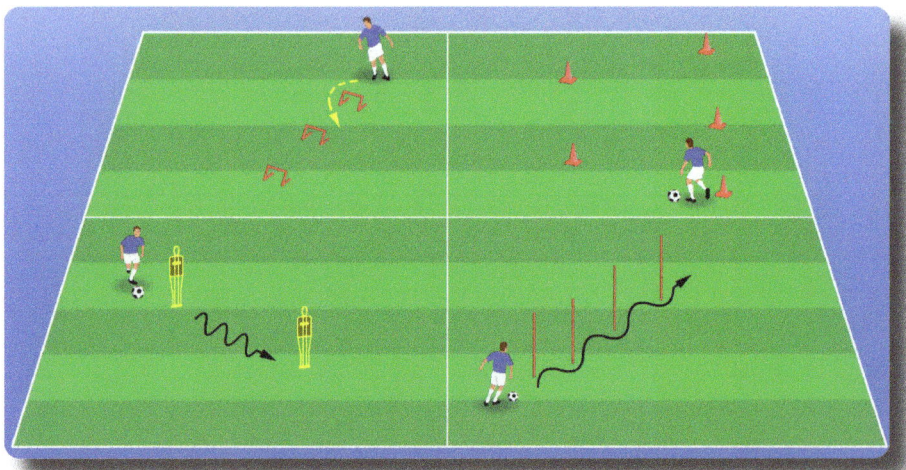

Image 76: *Low intensity aerobic drills with ball (technique) for the group that participated in game.*

Day 3 • Tuesday

- 1 x 10′ aerobic exercise (running at 75% MHR) - (see image 77).

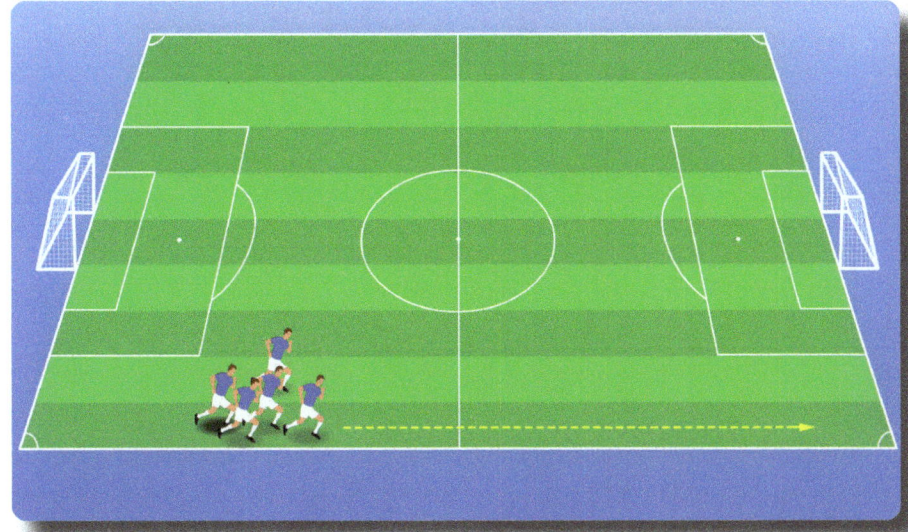

Image 77: *Low intensity aerobic running.*

- 1 x 10′ recovery strategies.

Group B (those who did not participate in the game on Sunday or participated for < 45 minutes on Sunday) follows the program below:

- 1 x 10′ general warm-up.
- 1 x 15′ specific warm-up.
- 4 x 4′ with 2′ stop. A simulation game with 4 vs 4 to 7 vs 7 players and 2 goalkeepers.
- Additional endurance/strength/speed training depending on the level and the needs of the non-starter players.
- 1 x 5′ low intensity running and cool off activity.

Afternoon: Rest

Planning

Day 4 • Wednesday

Morning:

- 1 x 10′ general warm-up (see image 78).

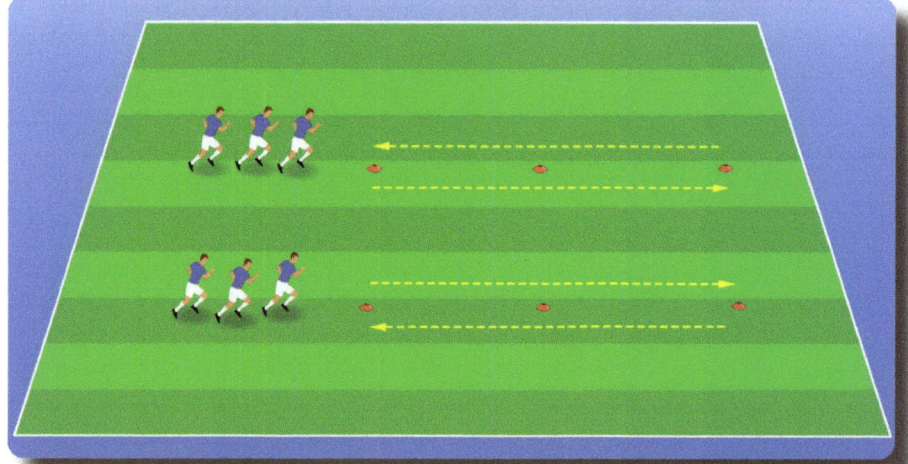

Image 78: *General warm-up drills.*

- 1 x 15′ specific warm-up (see image 79).

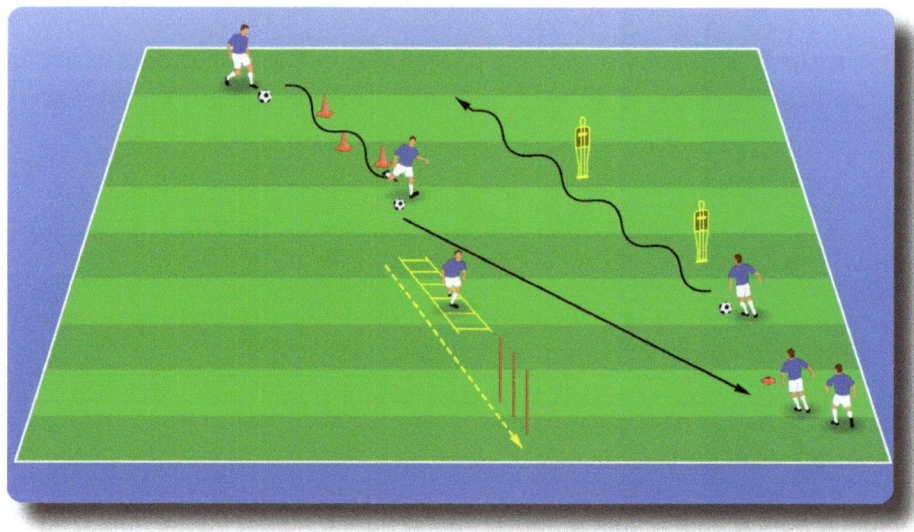

Image 79: *Specific warm-up drills.*

Day 4 • Wednesday

- 2 x 4 repetitions acceleration speed training (see image 80).

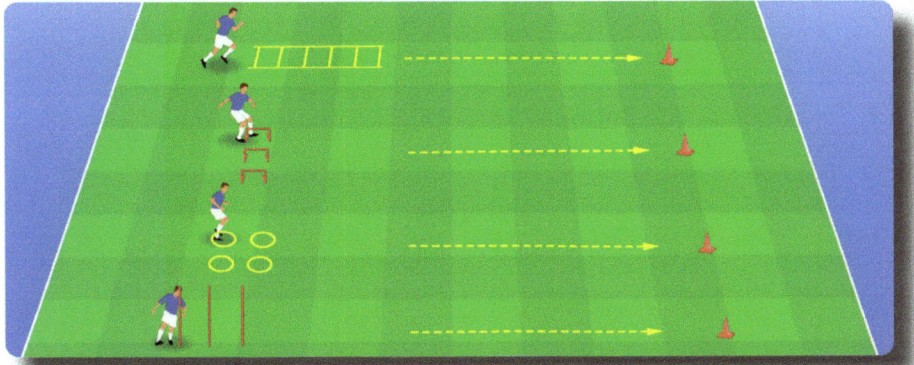

Image 80: *Acceleration speed drills.*

- 4 x 4' with 2' stop, game simulation exercise with 2 goalkeepers (see image 81).

Image 81: *Small-sided game, 5 vs 5 with 2 goalkeepers.*

- 1 x 5´ recovery strategies.

Afternoon:

- 1 x 10´ general warm-up.
- 1 x 30´ strength training (see strength section for references to this specific training unit).
- 1 x 5´ static stretching.

Planning

Day 5 • Thursday

Morning: 1 x 10´ general warm-up (see image 82).

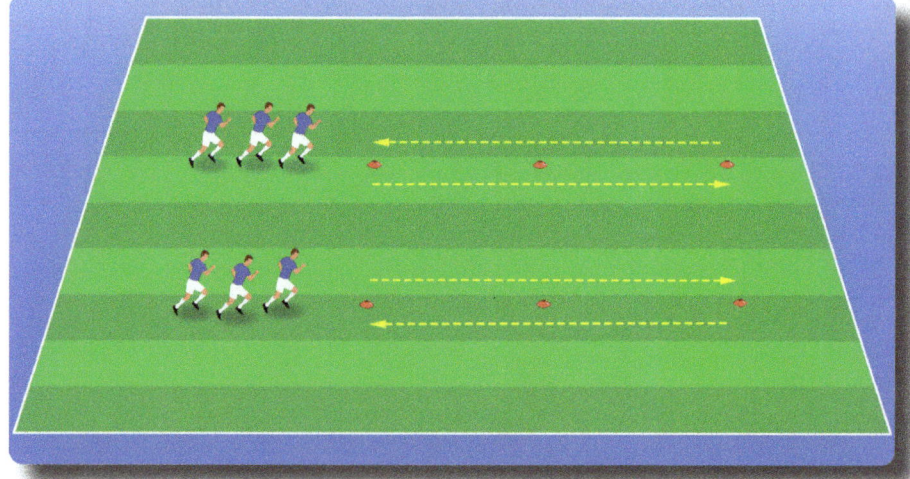

Image 82: *General warm-up drills.*

- 1 x 10´ specific warm-up with game simulation exercises 5 vs 2 (see image 83).

Image 83: *Rondo 5 vs 2.*

Day 5 • Thursday

- 2 x 10′ specific tactical training 11 vs 11 in the entire pitch with defensive and offensive game scenarios analysis (see image 84).

Image 84: *Specific tactical training.*

- 2-3 x 10′ with 2′ break free game 11 vs 11 at ⅔ or ¾ pitch (see image 85).

Image 85: *Free game 11 vs 11 at ⅔ pitch.*

- 1 x 5′ recovery strategies.

Afternoon: Rest

Planning

Day 6 • Friday

Morning:

- 1 x 15′ general warm-up (see image 86).

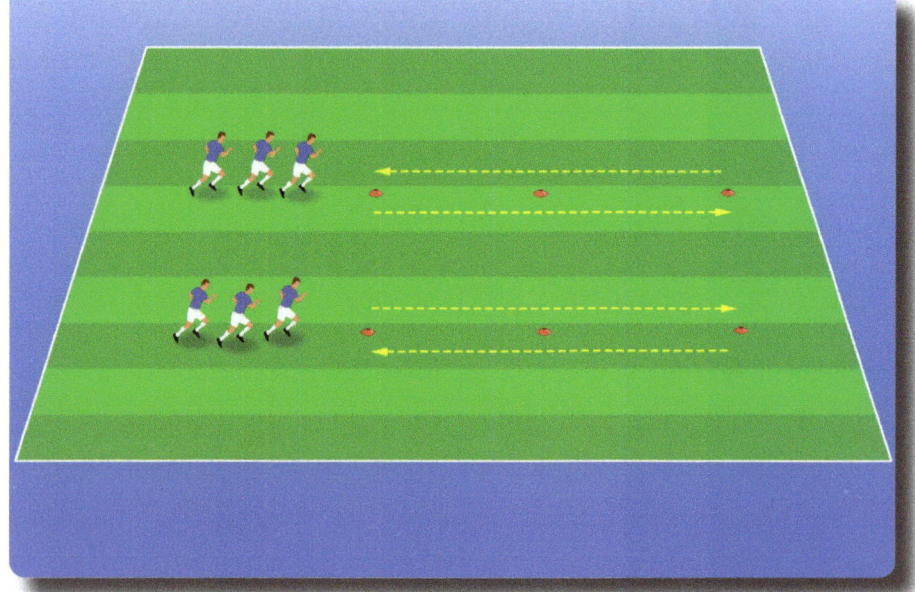

Image 86: *General warm-up drills.*

- 2 sets x 4 repetitions reaction speed training (see image 87).

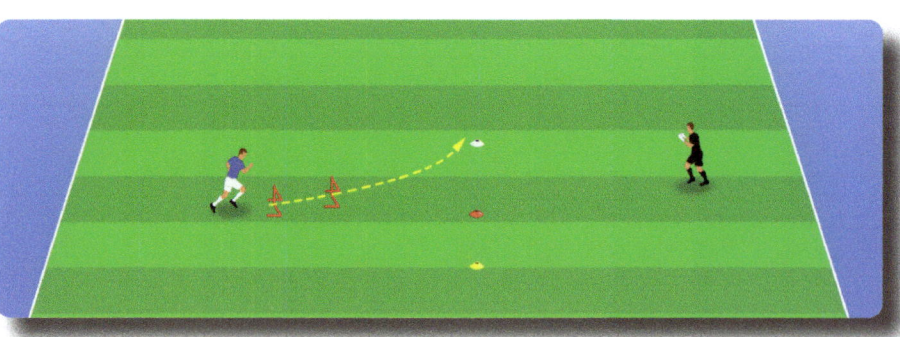

Image 87: *Acceleration and reaction speed drills.*

Day 6 • Friday

- 1 x 10´ technical training (variable), passing drills (see image 88).

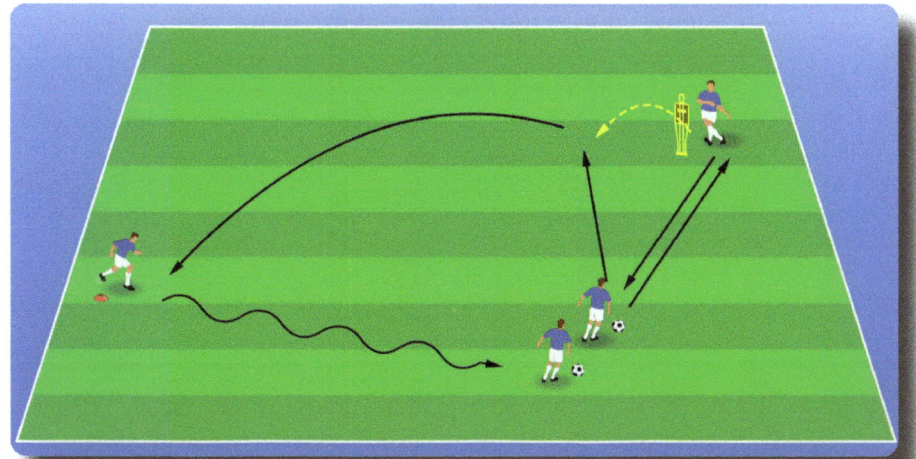

Image 88: *Passing drills.*

- 1 x 15´ finishing drills (see image 89).

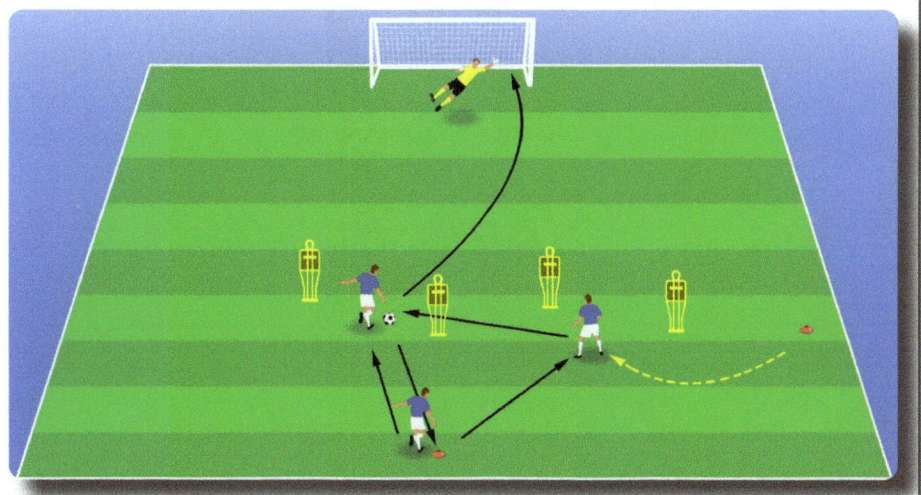

Image 89: *Technical/tactical drills with finishings.*

- 1 x 5´ recovery strategies.   **Afternoon:** Rest

Planning

Day 7 • Saturday

Morning:

- 1 x 10′ general warm-up (see image 90).

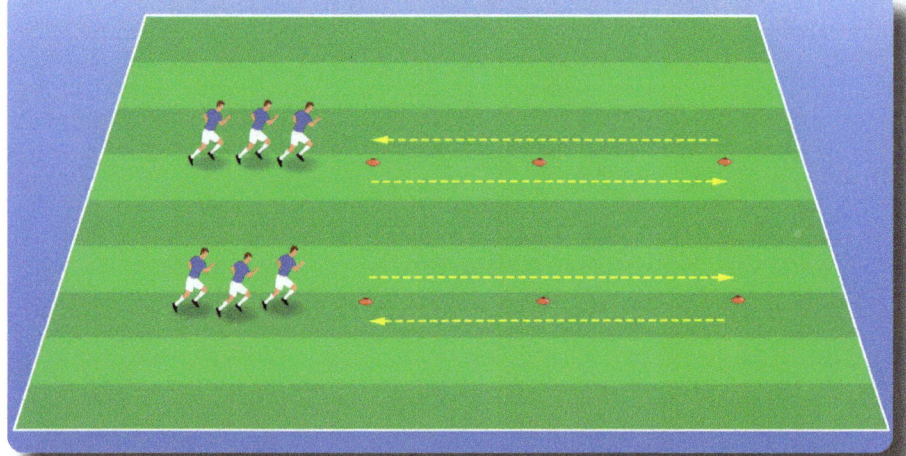

Image 90: *General warm-up drills.*

- 1 x 10′ specific warm-up (see image 91).

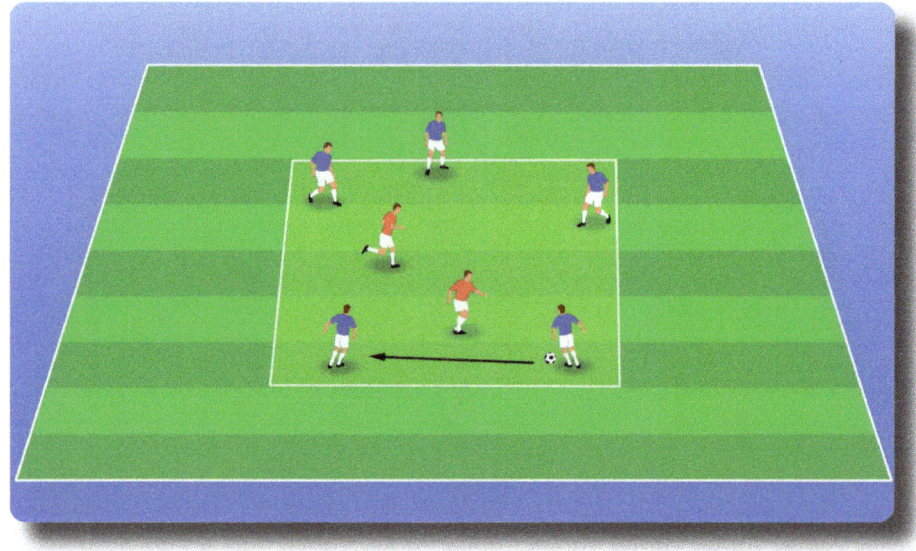

Image 90: *Rondo 5 vs 2.*

Day 7 • Saturday

- 4 x 2' with 1' break, 11 vs 11 game and defensive-offensive set pieces drills in ½ the field (see image 92).

Image 92: *Game simulation drills with set pieces.*

Afternoon: Rest

Example of a complete weekly micro cycle for the Maintenance Block

Day 1 • Sunday

Morning: Rest
Afternoon: Game

Day 2 • Monday

Day Off

Note: Day 2 and Day 3 can be reversed. Meaning that Monday can be the Day Off and Tuesday training in two groups or Tuesday can be the Day Off and Monday training in two groups.

Planning

Day 3 • Tuesday

Morning: Group A (those who participated in the game for > 45 minutes)
- 1 x 10´ general warm up (see image 93).

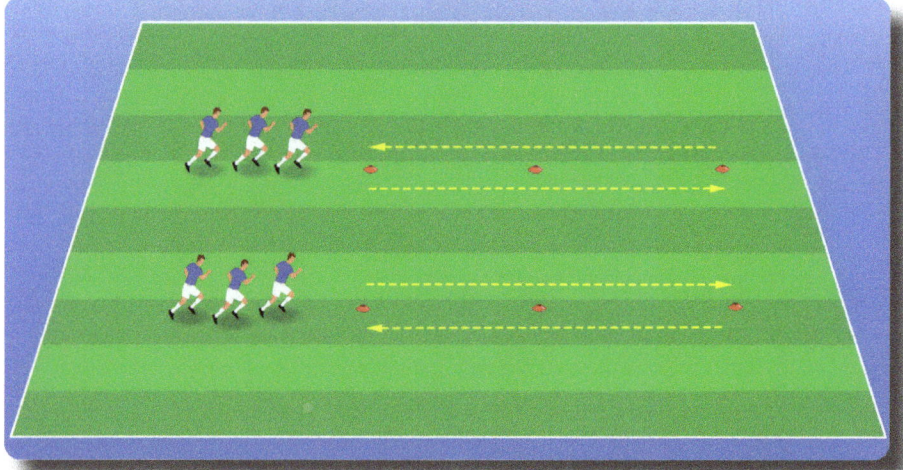

Image 93: *General warm-up drills.*

- 1 x 10´ flexibility and agility exercises.
- 1 x 10´ aerobic exercises with ball (technique) - (see image 94).

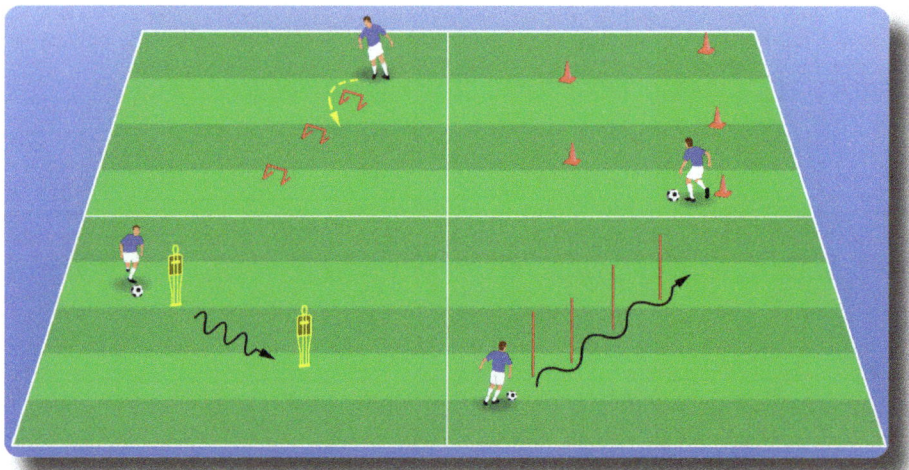

Image 94: *Low intensity aerobic drills with ball (technique) for the group that participated in game.*

Day 3 • Tuesday

- 1 x 10´ aerobic exercise (running at 75% MHR) - (see image 95).

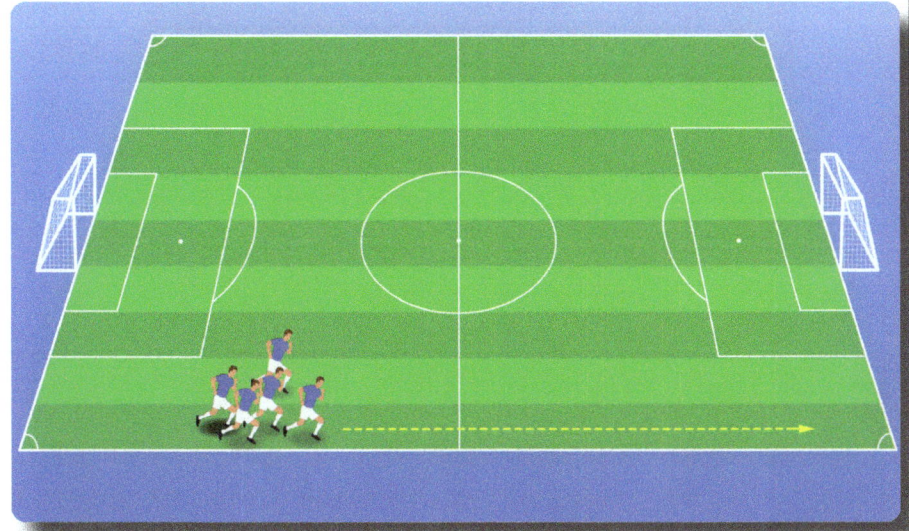

Image 95: *Low intensity aerobic running.*

- 1 x 10´ recovery strategies.

Group B (those who did not participate in the game on Sunday or participated for < 45 minutes on Sunday) follows the program below:

- 1 x 10´ general warm-up.
- 1 x 15´ specific warm-up.
- 4 x 4' with 2´ stops, simulation game with 4 vs 4 to 7 vs 7 players and 2 goalkeepers.
- Additional endurance/strength/speed training depending on the level and the needs of the non-starter players.
- 1 x 5´ low intensity running and cool off activity.

Afternoon: Rest

Planning

Day 4 • Wednesday

Morning:

- 1 x 10´ general warm-up (see image 96).

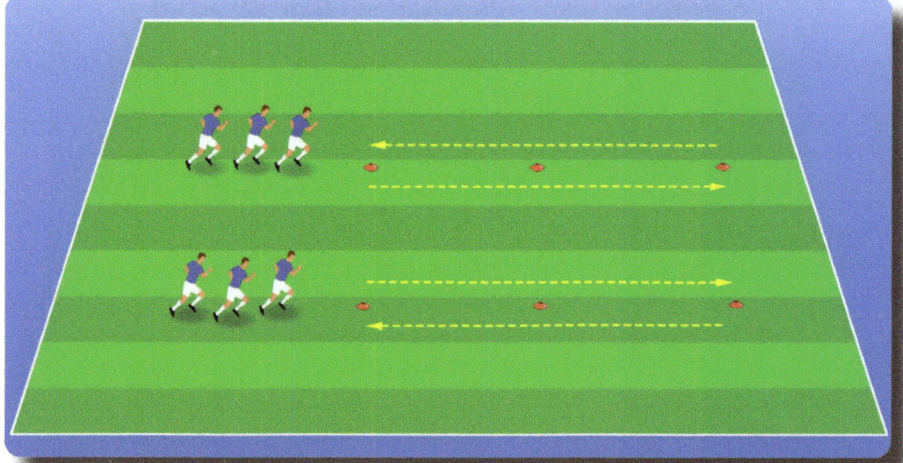

Image 96: *General warm-up drills.*

- 1 x 15´ specific warm-up (see image 97).

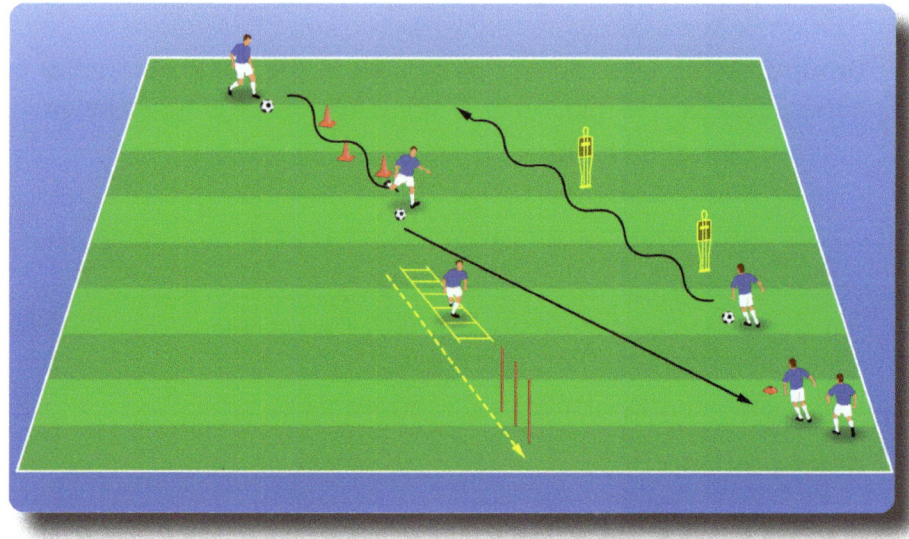

Image 97: *Specific warm-up drills.*

Day 4 • Wednesday

- 4 x 4' with 2' stop, game simulation exercise with 2 goalkeepers (see image 98).

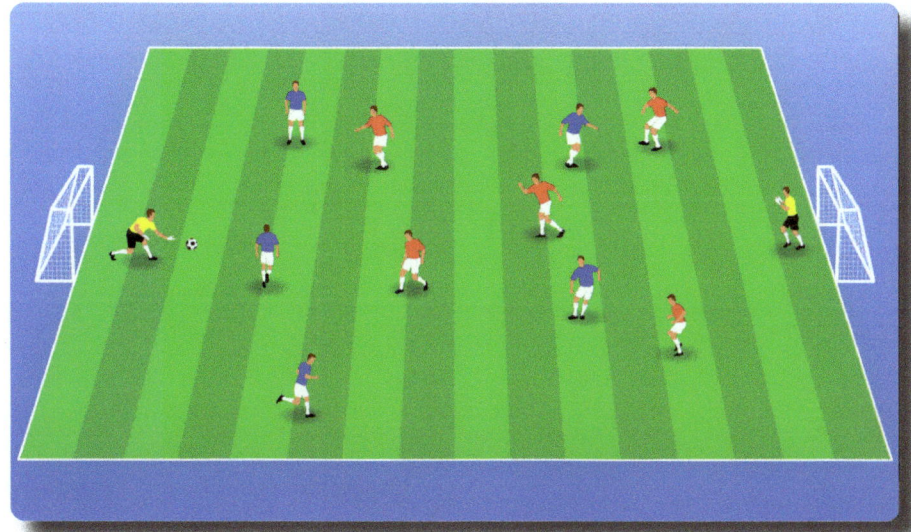

Image 98: *Small-sided game, 5 vs 5 with 2 goalkeepers.*

- 1 x 5´ low intensity running and cool off activity.

Afternoon:
- 1 x 10´ general warm-up.
- 1 x 30´ strength training (see strength section for references to this specific training unit).
- 1 x 5´ recovery strategies.

Planning

Day 5 • Thursday

Morning:
- 1 x 10′ general warm-up (see image 99).

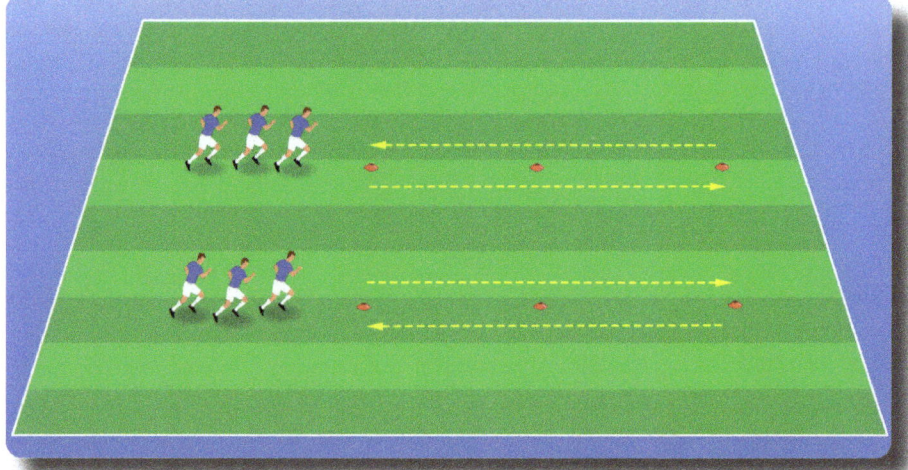

Image 99: *General warm-up exercises.*

- 1 x 10′ specific warm-up with game simulation drills 9 vs 3 (see image 100).

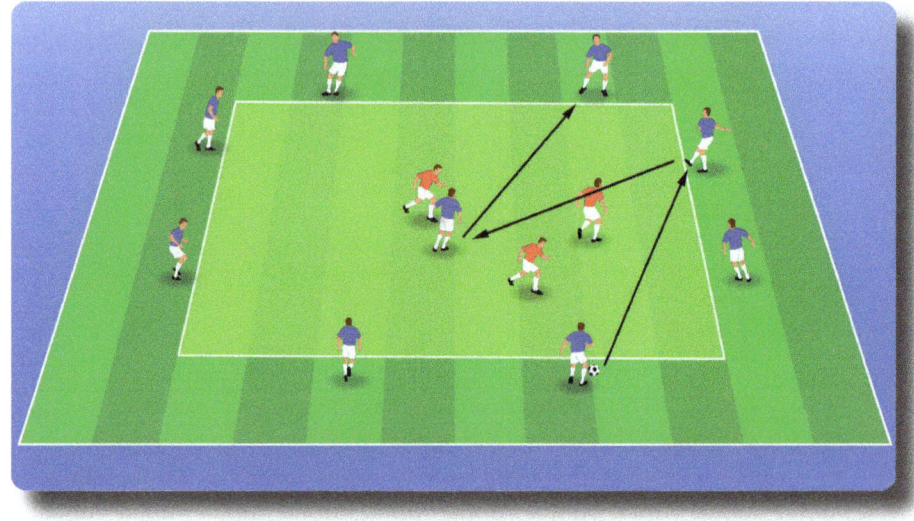

Image 100: *Game simulation drills 9 vs 3 for specific warm-up.*

Day 5 • Thursday

- 2 x 10′ specific tactical training 11 vs 11 in the entire pitch with defensive and offensive game scenarios analysis (see image 101).

Image 101: *Specific tactical training.*

- 2-3 x 10′ with 2′ break free game 11 vs 11 at ⅔ or ¾ pitch (see image 102).

Image 102: *Free game 11 vs 11 at ⅔ pitch.*

- 1 x 5′ recovery strategies.

Afternoon: Rest

Planning

Day 6 • Friday

Morning:

- 1 x 15´ general warm-up (see image 103).

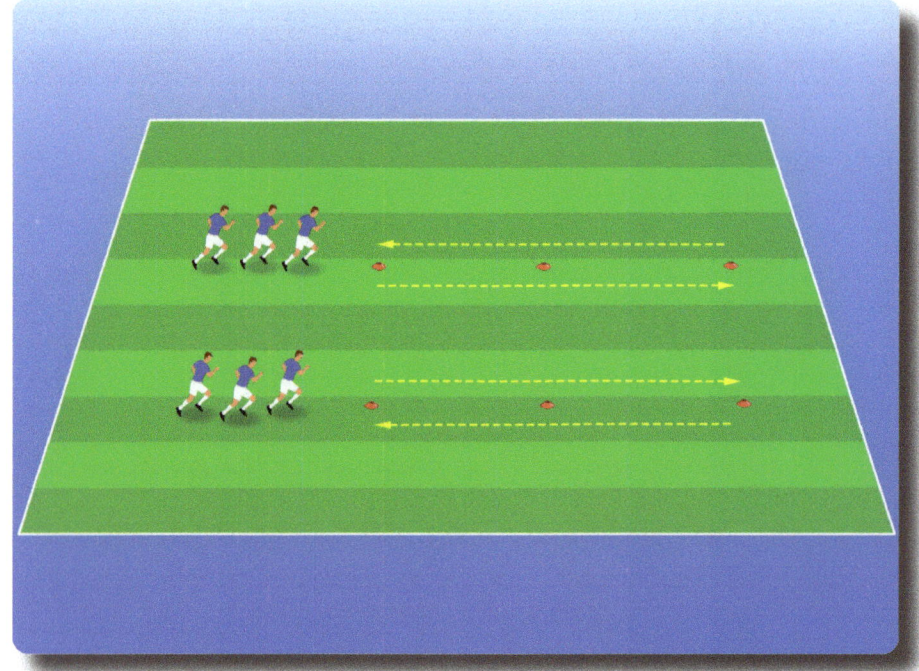

Image 103: *General warm-up drills.*

Day 6 • Friday

- 1 x 10′ technical training (variable), passing drills (see image 104).

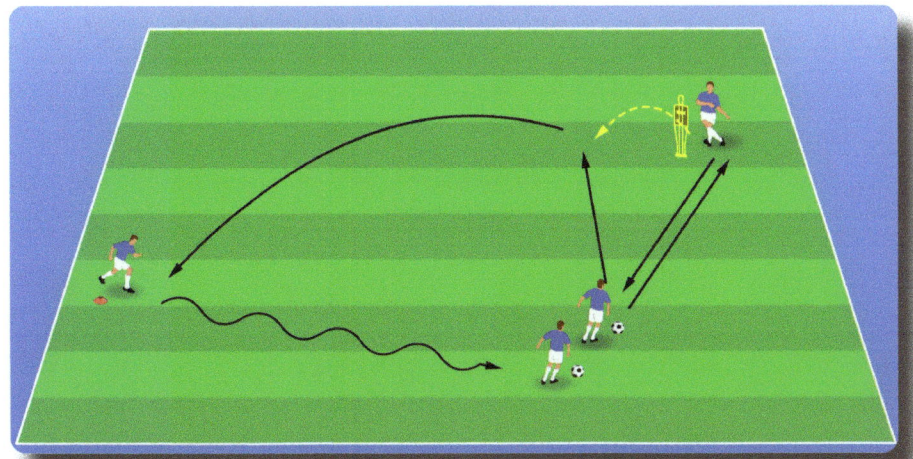

Image 104: *Passing drills.*

- 1 x 15′ finishing drills (see image 105).

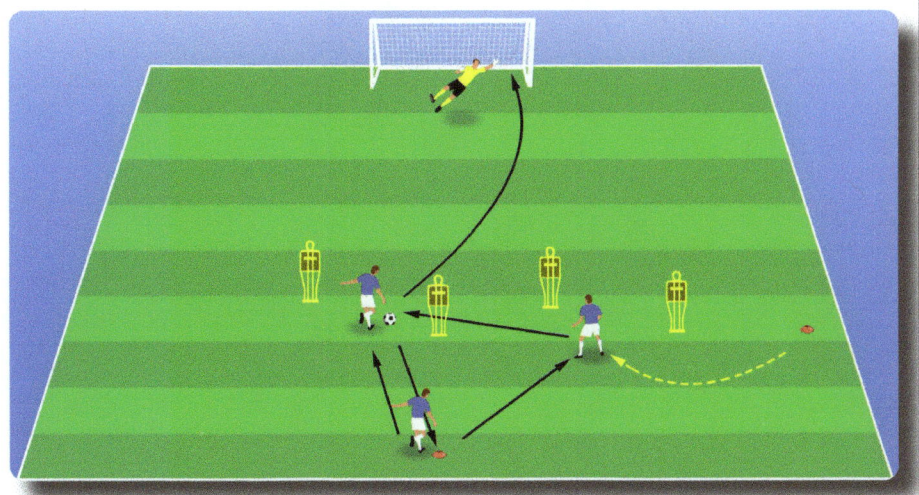

Image 105: *Technical/tactical drills with finishings.*

- 1 x 5′ recovery strategies. **Afternoon:** Rest

Planning

Day 7 • Saturday

Morning:

- 1 x 10´ general warm-up (see image 106).

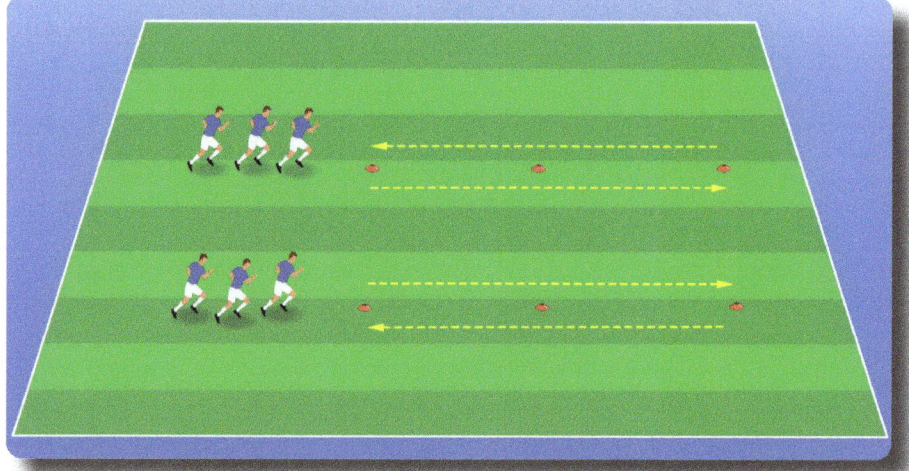

Image 106: *General warm-up drills.*

- 1 x 10´ specialised warm-up (see image 107).

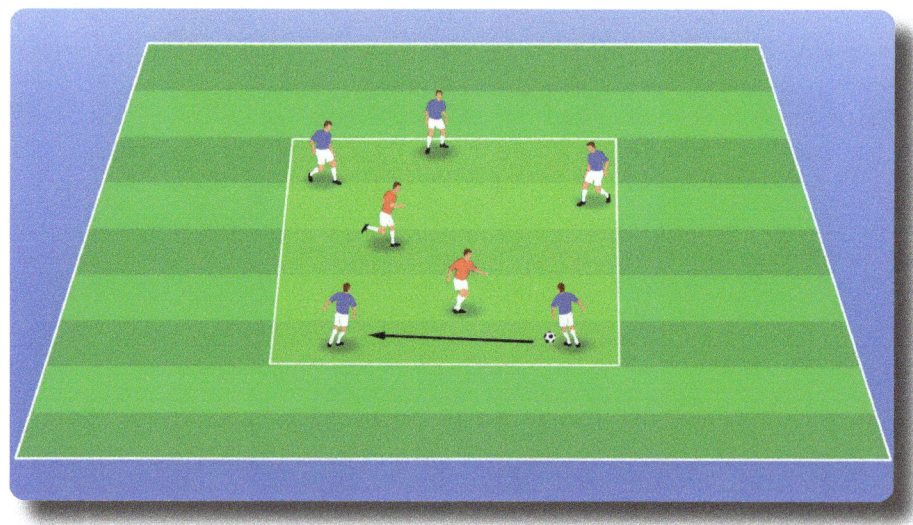

Image 107: *Game simulation drill 5 vs 2.*

Day 7 • Saturday

- 2 sets x 4 repetitions reaction speed (see image 108).

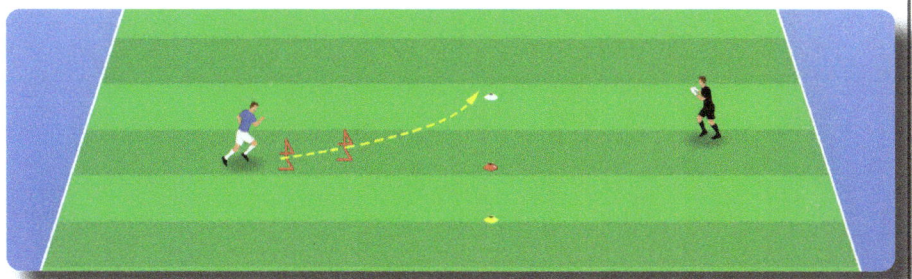

Image 108: *Acceleration and reaction speed training drill.*

- 4 x 2′ with 1′ break, 11 vs 11 game, defensive and offensive set pieces in ½ pitch (see image 109).

Image 109: *Game simulation drills with set pieces.*

Afternoon: Rest

Example of a complete weekly micro cycle for the Recovery Block

Day 1 • Sunday

Morning: Rest
Afternoon: Game

Day 2 • Monday

Day Off

Note: Day 2 and Day 3 can be reversed. Meaning that Monday can be the Day Off and Tuesday training in two groups or Tuesday can be the Day Off and Monday training in two groups.

Planning

Day 3 • Tuesday

Morning: Group A (those who participated in the game for > 45 minutes)
- 1 x 10´ general warm up (see image 110).

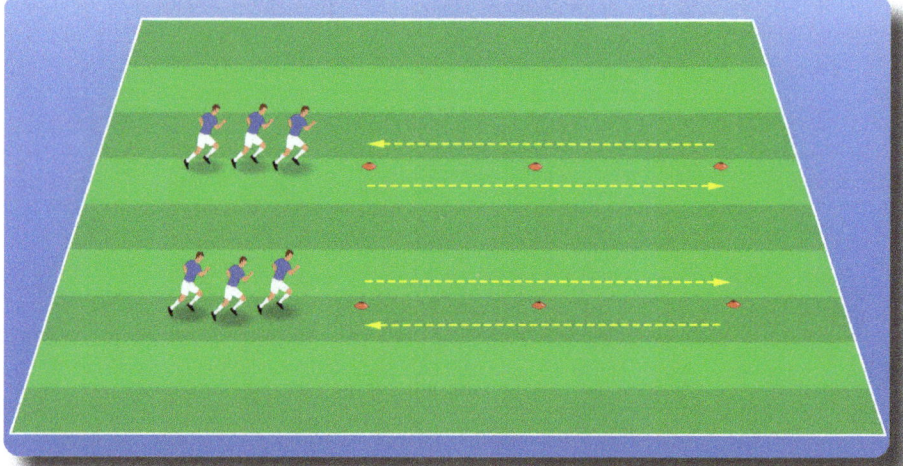

Image 110: *General warm-up drills.*

- 1 x 10´ flexibility and agility exercises.
- 1 x 10´ aerobic exercises with ball (technique) - (see image 111).

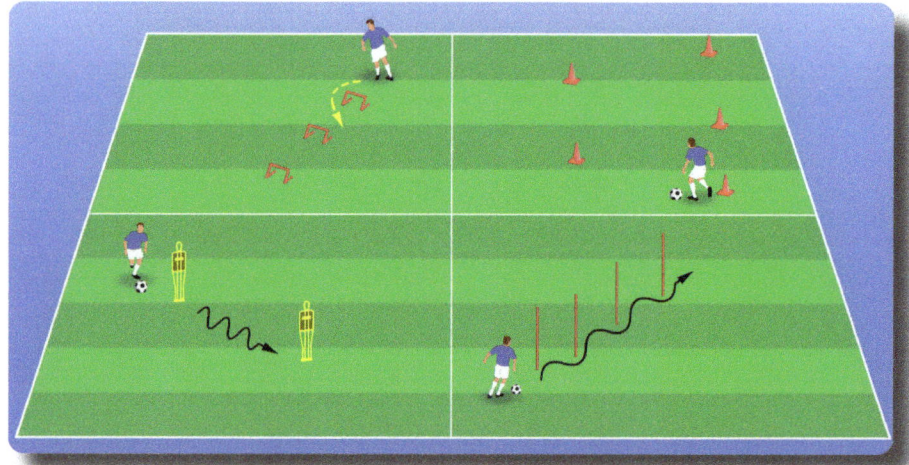

Image 111: *Low intensity aerobic drills with ball (technique) for the group that participated in game.*

Day 3 • Tuesday

- 1 x 10′ aerobic exercise (running at 75% MHR) - (see image 112).

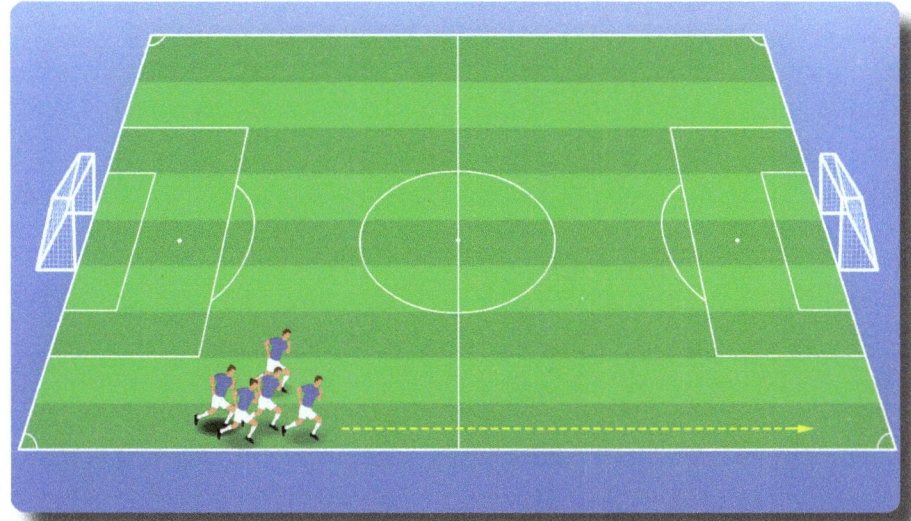

Image 112: *Low intensity aerobic running.*

- 1 x 10′ recovery strategies.

Group B (those who did not participate in the game on Sunday or participated for < 45 minutes on Sunday) follows the program below:

- 1 x 10′ general warm-up.
- 1 x 15′ specific warm-up.
- 4 x 4′ with 2′ stops, simulation game with 4 vs 4 to 7 vs 7 players and 2 goalkeepers.
- Additional endurance/strength/speed training depending on the level and the needs of the non-starter players.
- 1 x 5′ low intensity running and cool off activity.

Afternoon: Rest

Planning

Day 4 • Wednesday

Morning:

- 1 x 10′ general warm-up (see image 113).

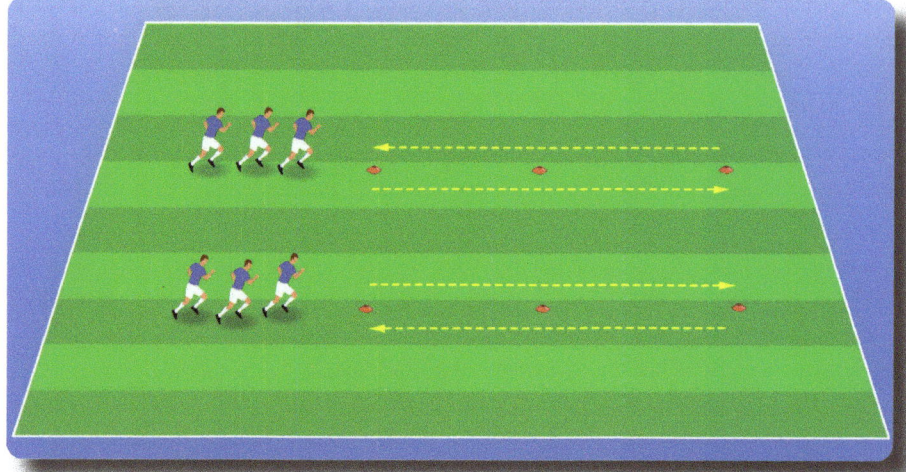

Image 113: *General warm-up drills.*

- 1 x 15′ specific warm-up (see image 114).

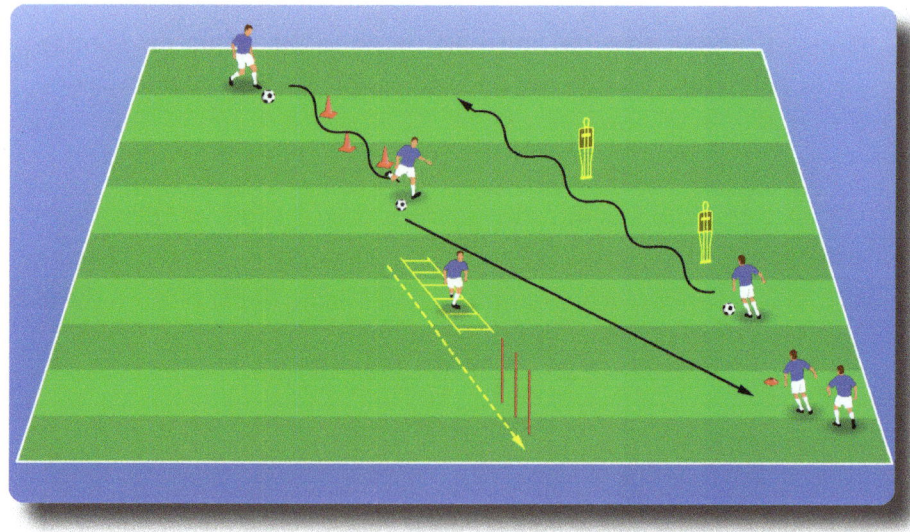

Image 114: *Specific warm-up drills.*

Day 4 • Wednesday

- 2-3 x 10´ with 2´ break free game 11 vs 11 at ⅔ or ¾ pitch (see image 115).

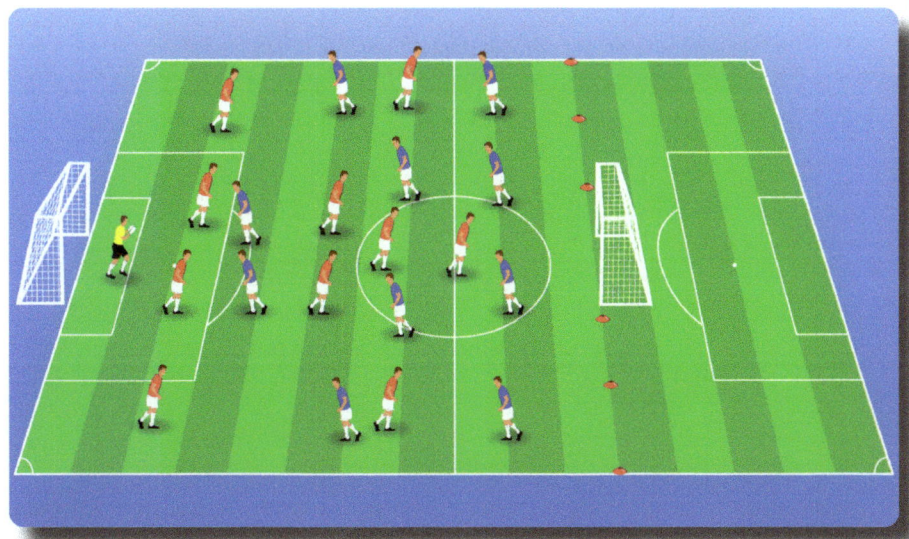

Image 115: *Free game 11 vs 11 at ⅔ pitch.*

- 1 x 5´ set pieces.

Afternoon: Rest

Planning

Day 5 • Thursday

Morning:

- 1 x 10′ general warm-up (see image 116).

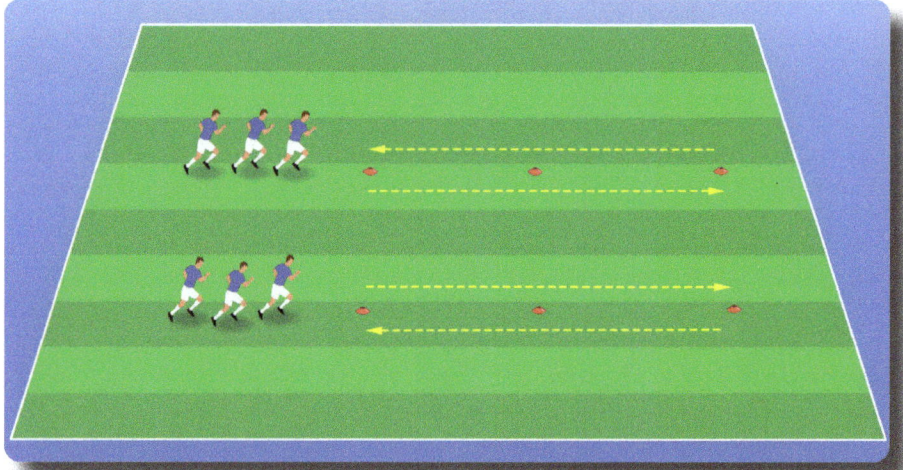

Image 116: *General warm-up drills.*

- 1 x 10′ specific warm-up with game simulation drills 9 vs 3 (see image

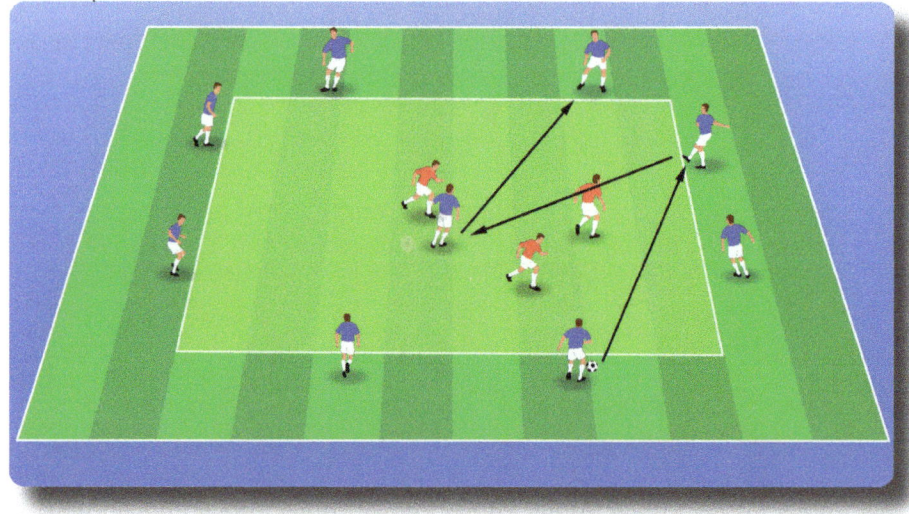

Image 117: *Game simulation drills 9 vs 3 for specific warm-up.*

Day 5 • Thursday

- 2 x 10′ specific tactical training 11 vs 11 in the entire pitch with defensive and offensive game scenarios analysis (see image 118).

Image 118: *Special tactics.*

- 2-3 x 10′ with 2′ break free game 11 vs 11 at ⅔ or 3/4 pitch (see image 119).

Image 119: *Free game 11 vs 11 at ⅔ pitch.*

- 1 x 5′ recovery strategies   **Afternoon:** Rest

Planning

Day 6 • Friday

Morning:

- 1 x 15′ general warm-up (see image 120).

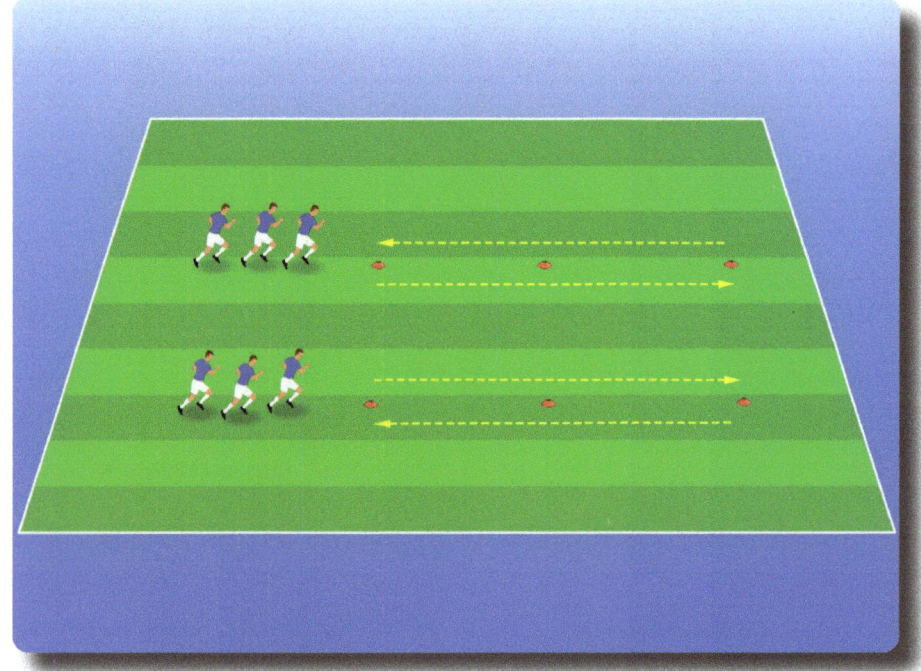

Image 120: *General warm-up drills.*

Day 6 • Friday

- 1 x 10′ technical training (variable), passing drills (see image 121).

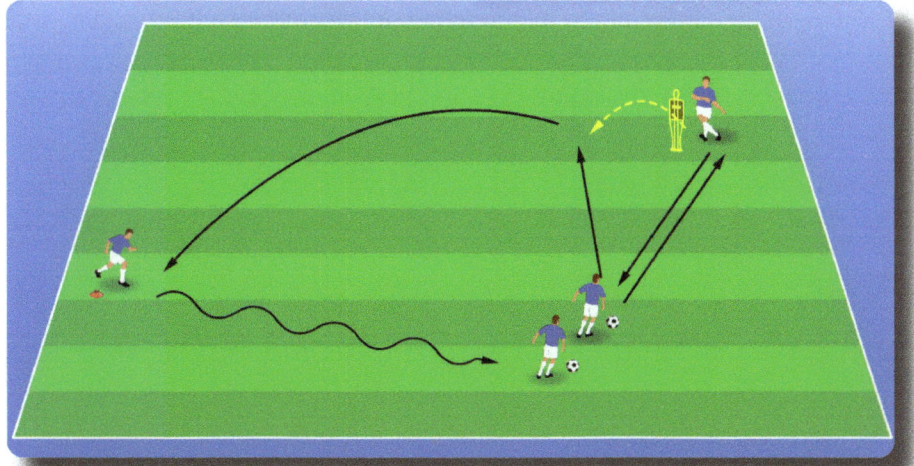

Image 121: *Passing drills.*

- 1 x 15′ exercise in finishes (see image 122)

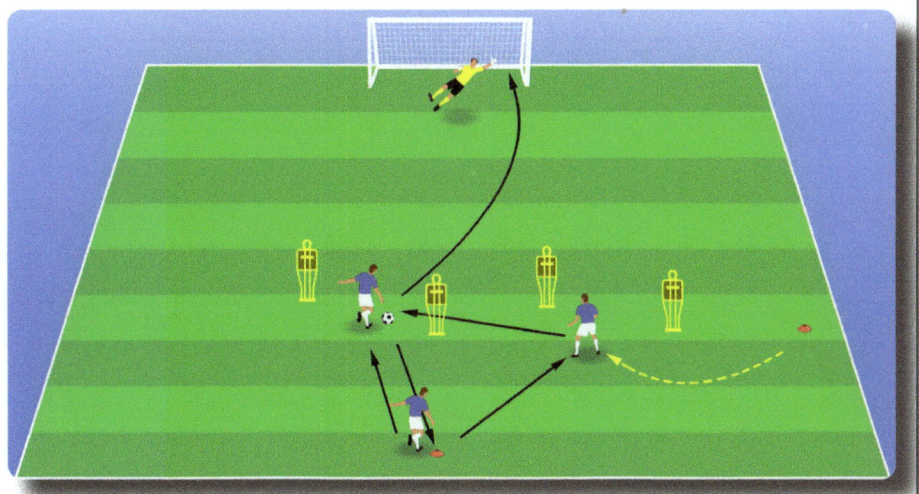

Image 122: *Technical/tactical drills with finishings.*

- 1 x 5′ recovery strategies   **Afternoon:** Rest

Planning

Day 7 • Saturday

Morning:

- 1 x 10′ general warm-up (see image 123).

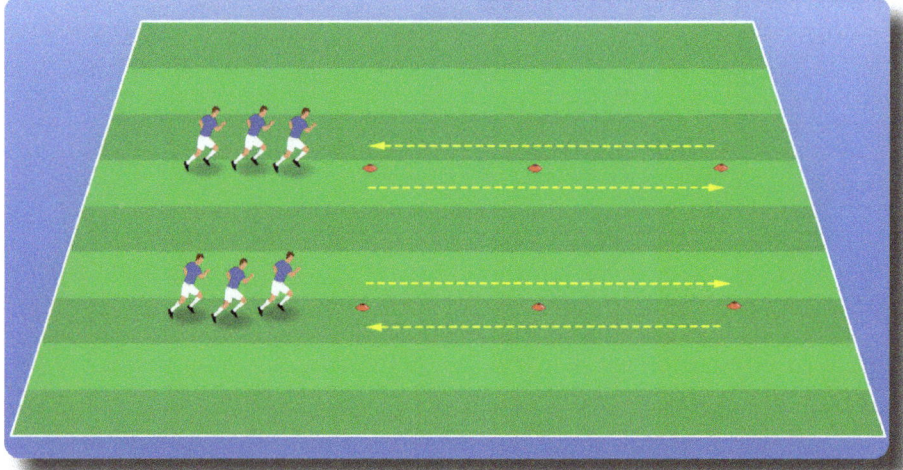

Image 123: *General warm-up drills.*

- 1 x 10′ specific warm-up (see image 124).

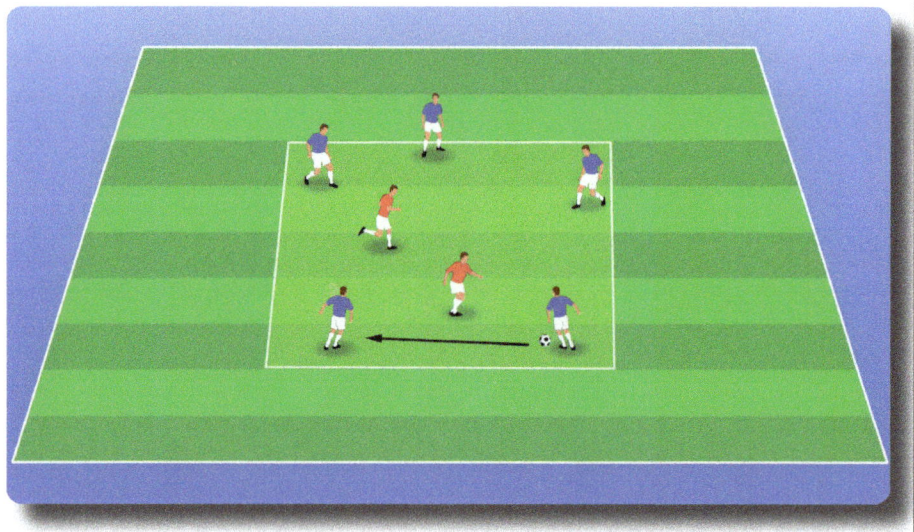

Image 124: *Rondo 5 vs 2.*

Day 7 • Saturday

- 1 set x 4 repetitions reaction speed training (see image 125)

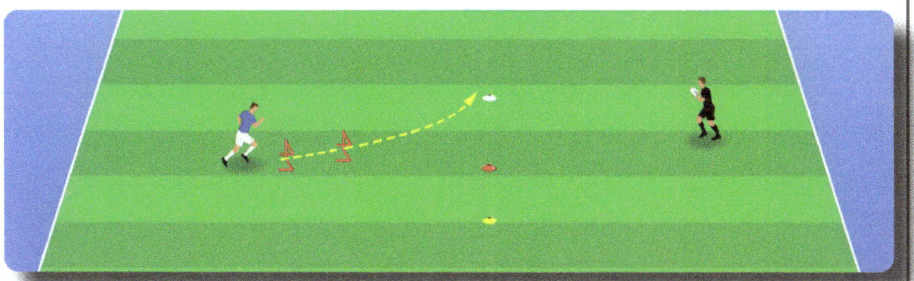

Image 125: *Acceleration and reaction speed training drill.*

- 4 x 2′ with 1′ break, 11 vs 11 game, offensive and defensive set in ½ the pitch (see image 126).

Image 126: *Game simulation drill with set pieces.*

Afternoon: Rest

BIBLIOGRAPHY

Asadi A, Arazi H, Young WB, Saez de Viallareal E. The effects of plyometric training on change of direction ability: a meta-analysis. Int J Sports Physiol Perform, 2016; 11: 563-73.

Bangsbo J, Iaia FM, Krustrup P. Metabolic response and fatigue in soccer. Int J Sports Physiol Perform, 2007; 2: 111-127.

Barnes C, Archer DT, Hogg B, Bush M, Bradley PS. The evolution of physical and technical performance parameters in the English Premier League. Int J Sports Med, 2014; 35: 1-6.

Barnes KR, Kilding AE. Strategies to improve running economy. Sports Med, 2015; 45: 37-56.

Bedoya AA, Milternberger MR, Lopez RM. Plyometric training effects on athletic performance in youth soccer players: a systematic review. J Strength Cond Res, 2015; 29: 2351-2360.

Bompa T, Buzzichelli C. Periodization training for sports, 3rd edition, 2015.

Bradley PS, Carling C, Archer D, Roberts J, Dodds A, Di Mascio M, Paul D, Diaz AG, Peart D, Krustrup P. The effect of playing formation on high-intensity running and technical profiles in English FA Premier League soccer matches. J Sports Sci, 2011; 29: 821-30.

Bradley PS, Lago-Penas C, Rey E, Gomez Diaz A. The effect of high and low percentage ball possession on physical and technical profiles in English FA Premier League soccer matches. J Sports Sci, 2013; 31: 1261-1270.

Bradley PS, Di Mascio M, Peart D, et al. High-intensity activity profiles of elite soccer players at different performance levels. J Strength Cond Res, 2010; 24: 2343-2351.

Bradley PS, Noakes TD. Match running performance fluctuations in elite soccer: Indicative of fatigue, pacing or situational influences? J Sports Sci, 2013; 31: 1627-1638.

Bradley PS, Sheldon W, Wooster B, et al. High-intensity running in English FA Premier League soccer matches. J Sports Sci, 2009; 27: 159-168.

Bush M, Barnes C, Archer DT, Hogg B, Bradley PS. Evolution of match performance parameters for various playing positions in the English Premier League. Hum Mov Sci, 2015; 39: 1-11.

Cardinale M, Varley MC. Wearable training-monitoring technology: Applications, challenges and opportunities. Int J Sports Physiol Perform, 2017; 12: S255-S262.

Carling C. Interpreting physical performance in professional soccer match-play: should we be more pragmatic in our approach? Sports Med, 2013; 43: 655-663.

Carling C, Dupont G. Are declines in physical performance associated with a reduction in skill-related performance during professional soccer match-play? J Sports Sci, 2011; 21: 63-67.

Chad, N. An approach to the periodisation of training during the in-season for team sports. Prof Strength Cond, 2010; 18: 5-10.

Cormie P, McGuigan MR, Newton RU. Adaptations in athletic performance following ballistic power vs strength training. Med Sci Sports Exerc, 2010a; 42: 1582-1598.

Cormie P, McGuigan MR, Newton RU. Influence of strength on magnitude and mechanisms of adaptation to power training. Med Sci Sports Exerc, 2010b, 42: 1566-1581.

Cormie P, McGuigan MR, Newton RU. Developing maximal neuromuscular power: part 2-training considerations for improving maximal power production. Sports Med, 2011; 41: 125-146.

Dajaoui L, Haddad M, Chamari K, Dellal A. Monitoring training load and fatigue with physiological markers. Physiol Behav, 2107; 81: 86-94.

Dellal A, Da Silva CD, Hill-Haas S, Del Wong P, Natali AJ, De Lima JR, Bara Filho MG, Marins JJ, Garcia ES, Chan K. Heart-rate monitoring in soccer: interest and limits during competitive match play and training, practical application. J Strength Cond Res, 2012; 26: 2890-2906.

Dellaserra CL, Gao Y, Ransdell L. Use of integrated technology in team sports: a review of opportunities, challenges and future directions for athletes. J Strength Cond Res, 2014; 28: 556-573.

Foster C, Rodriguez-Marroyo JA, de Koning JJ. Monitoring training loads: the past, the present, and the future. Int J Sports Physiol Perform, 2017; 12: S227-S234.

Gamble P. Training for sports speed and agility: An evidence-based approach, 2011.

Gamble, P. Periodization of training for team sports athletes. Strength Cond J, 2006; 28: 56-66.

Gamble P. A skill-based conditioning games approach to metabolic conditioning for elite rugby football players. J Strength Cond Res, 2004; 18: 491-497.

Gregson W, Drust B, Atkinson G, Di Salvo V. Match-to-match variability of high-speed activities in Premier League soccer. Int J Sports Med, 2010; 31: 237-242.

Haff GG, Nimphius S. Training principles for power. Strength Cond J, 2012; 34: 2-12.

Halson SL. Monitoring training load to understand fatigue in athletes. Sports Med, 2014; 44: S139-S147.

Jones CM, Griffiths PC, Mallalieu SD. Training load and fatigue marker associations with injury and illness: A systematic review of longitudinal studies. Sports Med, 2017; 47: 943-974.

Kraemer WJ, French DN, Paxton NJ, Hakkinen K, Volek JS, Sebastianelli WJ, et al. Changes in exercise performance and hormonal concentrations over a big ten soccer season in starters and nonstarters. J Strength Cond Res, 2004; 18: 121-128.

Little T. Optimizing the use of football drills for physiological development. J Strength Cond Res, 2009; 31: 67-74.

Little T, Williams AG. Specificity of acceleration, maximal speed and agility in professional soccer players. J Strength Cond Res, 2005; 19: 76-78.

Lopez-Segovia M, Palao Andres JM, Gonzalez-Badillo JJ. Effect of 4 months of training on aerobic power, strength, and acceleration in two under-19 soccer teams. J Strength Cond Res, 2010; 24: 2705-2714.

Mallo J. Effect of block periodization on physical fitness during a competitive soccer season. Intl J Perfor Anal Sport, 2012; 12: 64-74.

Malone JJ, Lovell R, Varley MC, Coutts AJ. Unpacking the black box: Apllications and considerations for using GPS devices in sport. Int J Sports Physiol Perform, 2017; 12: S218-S226.

Markovic G. Does plyometric training improve vertical jump height? A meta-analytical review. Br J Sports Med, 2007; 39: 1051-1060.

Morgans R, Orme P, Anderson L, Drust B. Principles and practices of training for soccer. J Sport Health Sci, 2014; 3: 251-257.

Papadakis L, Patras K, Georgoulis AD. In-season concurrent aerobic endurance and CMJ improvements are feasible for both starters and non-starters in professional soccer players: A case study. J Aust Strength Cond, 2015; 23: 19-30.

Peterson MD, Rhea MR, Alvar BA. Maximising strength development in athletes: A meta-analysis to determine the dose-response relationship. J Strength Cond Res, 2004; 18: 377-382.

Rampinini E, Coutts AJ, Castagna C, et al. Variation in top level soccer match performance. Int J Sports Med, 2007; 28: 1018-1024.

Rampinini E, Impellizzeri FM, Castagna C, et al. Technical performance during soccer matches of the Italian Serie A league: effect of fatigue and competitive level. J Sci Med Sport, 2009; 12: 227-233.

Rønnestad BR, Nymark BS, Raastad T. Effects of in-season strength maintenance training frequency in professional soccer players. J Strength Cond Res, 2011; 25: 2653-2660.

Rumpf M, Lockie RG, Cronin JB, Jalivand F. Effect of different sprint training methods on sprint performance over various distances: a brief review. J Strength Cond Res, 2016; 30: 1767-1785.

Di Salvo V, Gregson W, Atkinson G, et al. Analysis of high intensity activity in Premier League soccer. Int J Sports Med, 2009; 30: 205-212.

Di Salvo V, Pigozzi F, Gonzalez-Haro C, Laughlin MS, De Witt JK. Match performance comparison in top English soccer leagues. Int J Sports Med, 2013; 34: 526-532.

Sands WA, Kavanaugh JD, Gastin PB. Modern techniques and technologies applied to training and performance monitoring. Int J Sports Physiol Perform, 2017; 12: S263-S272.

Silva JR, Magalhaes JF, Ascensao AA, Oliveira EM, Seabra AF, Rebelo AN. Individual match playing time during the season affects fitness-related parameters of male professional soccer players. J Strength Cond Res, 2011; 25: 2729-2739.

Stone MH, Moir G, Glaister M, Snaders R. How much strength is necessary? Phy Ther Sport, 2002; 3: 88-96.

Tierney PJ, Young A, Clarke ND, Duncan MJ. Match play demands of 11 versus 11 professional football using Global Positioning System tracking: Variations across common playing formations. Hum Mov Sci, 2016; 49: 1-8.

Turner AN. Training for power: principles and practice. Prof Strength Cond, 2009; 14: 20-32.

Turner AN, Stewart PF. Strength and conditioning for soccer players. Strength Cond J, 2014; 36: 1-13.

Viru A, Viru M. Biochemical monitoring of sport training, 2000.

Van Winckel J, McMillan K, Buzzichelli C, Tenney D, Bradley P. Periodization in soccer. In: Fitness in soccer: The science and practical application, 2014.

Yule, S. Maintaining an in-season conditioning edge. In: High-Performance Training for Sports, 2014.

www.ingramcontent.com/pod-product-compliance
Lightning Source LLC
Chambersburg PA
CBHW041237240426
43661CB00066B/2907